D0468108

BEHIND THE SCENES AT THE SPACE STATIONS

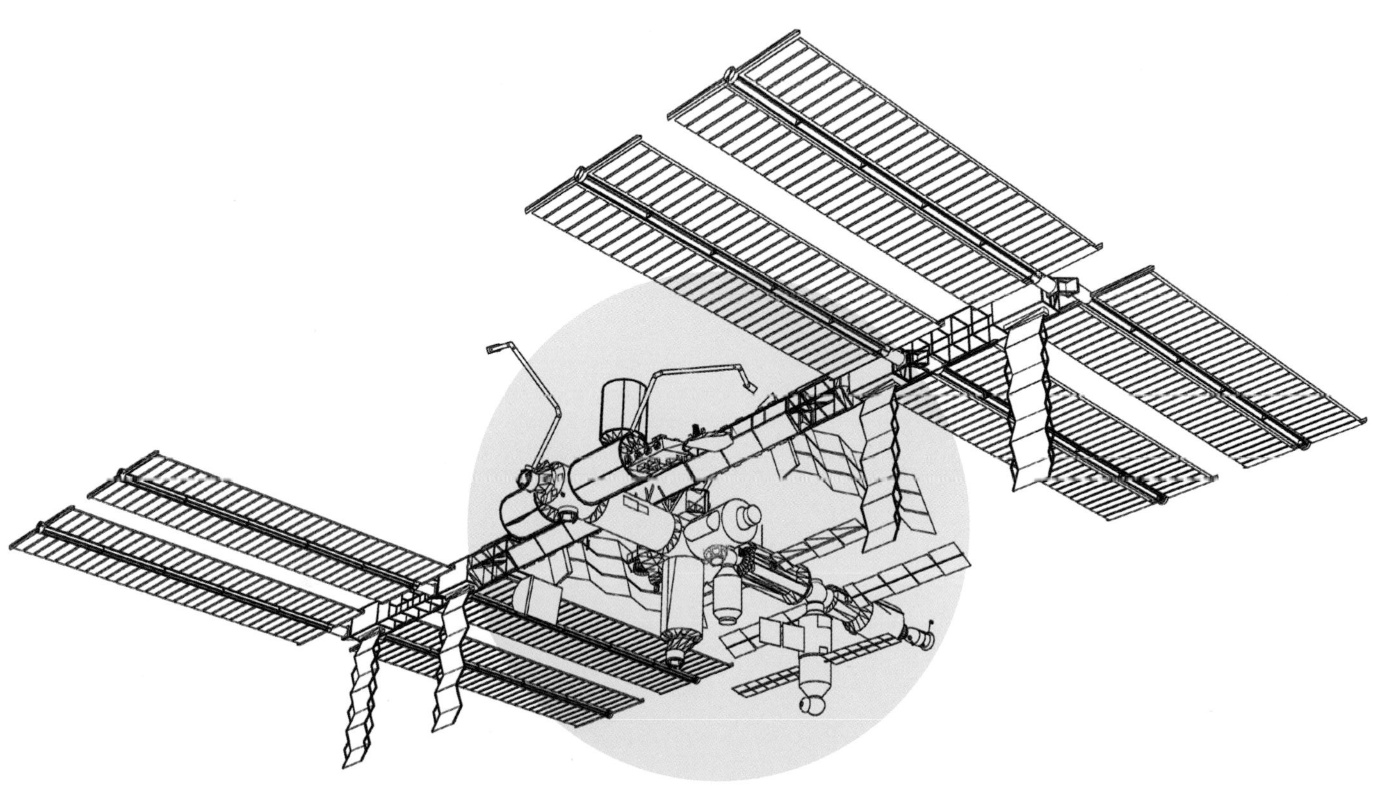

DK SMITHSONIAN

BEHIND THE SCENES AT THE SPACE STATIONS

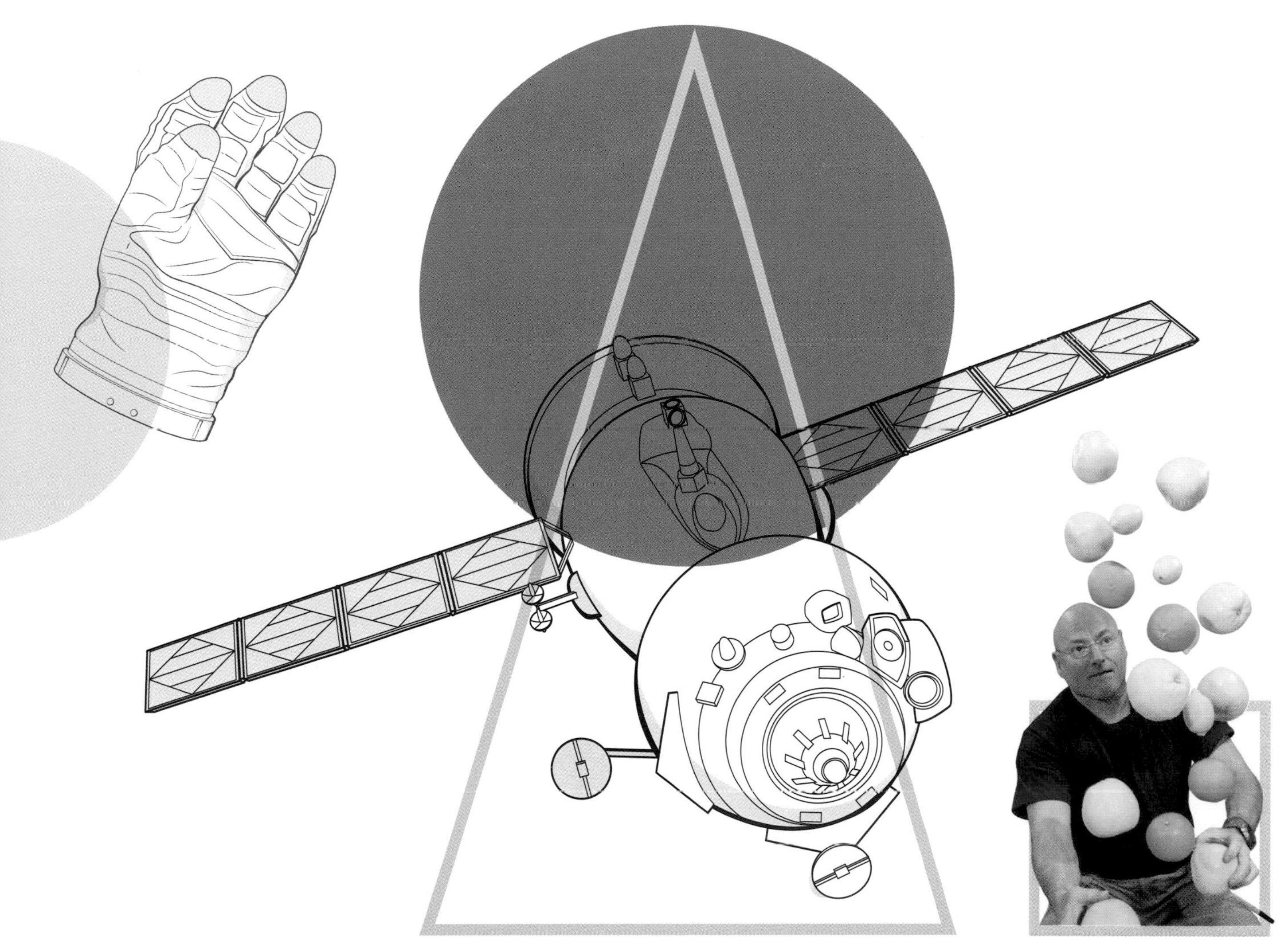

EXPERIENCE LIFE IN SPACE

Senior Editor Amanda Wyatt **Project Art Editor** Joe Lawrence
Editor Edward Aves **US Editor** Heather Wilcox
Writers Giles Sparrow, Vijay Shah
Consultant Dr. Suzie Imber
Picture Researchers Sarah Hopper, Sarah Smithies
Managing Editor Rachel Fox **Managing Art Editor** Owen Peyton Jones
Production Editor Jacqueline Street-Elkayam
Senior Production Controller Meskerem Berhane
Illustrator Peter Bull **Jacket Designer** Akiko Kato
Publisher Andrew Macintyre **Art Director** Karen Self
Associate Publishing Director Liz Wheeler
Publishing Director Jonathan Metcalf

DK DELHI

Senior Editor Dharini Ganesh **Senior Art Editor** Devika Dwarkadas
Project Editor Priyanjali Narain **Senior DTP Designer** Harish Aggarwal
DTP Designers Jaypal Singh Chauhan, Rajdeep Singh
Jacket Designer Juhi Sheth **Senior Jackets Editorial Coordinator** Priyanka Sharma
Senior Managing Editor Rohan Sinha **Managing Art Editor** Sudakshina Basu
Pre-production Manager Balwant Singh **Production Manager** Pankaj Sharma
Editorial Head Glenda Fernandes **Design Head** Malavika Talukder

First American Edition, 2022
Published in the United States by DK Publishing
1450 Broadway, Suite 801, New York, NY 10018

22 23 24 25 26 10 9 8 7 6 5 4 3 2 1
001–326784–May/2022

A catalog record for this book is available from the Library of Congress.
ISBN 978-0-7440-5610-5

DK books are available at special discounts when purchased in bulk for sales promotions, premiums, fund-raising, or educational use. For details contact:
DK Publishing Special Markets,
1450 Broadway, Suite 801, New York, NY 10018 or SpecialSales@dk.com

Printed and bound in China

For the curious
www.dk.com

Established in 1846, the Smithsonian is the world's largest museum and research complex, dedicated to public education, national service, and scholarship in the arts, sciences, and history. It includes 19 museums and galleries and the National Zoological Park. The total number of artifacts, works of art, and specimens in the Smithsonian's collection is estimated at 156 million.

This book was made with Forest Stewardship Council ™ certified paper—one small step in DK's commitment to a sustainable future. For more information, go to www.dk.com/our-green-pledge.

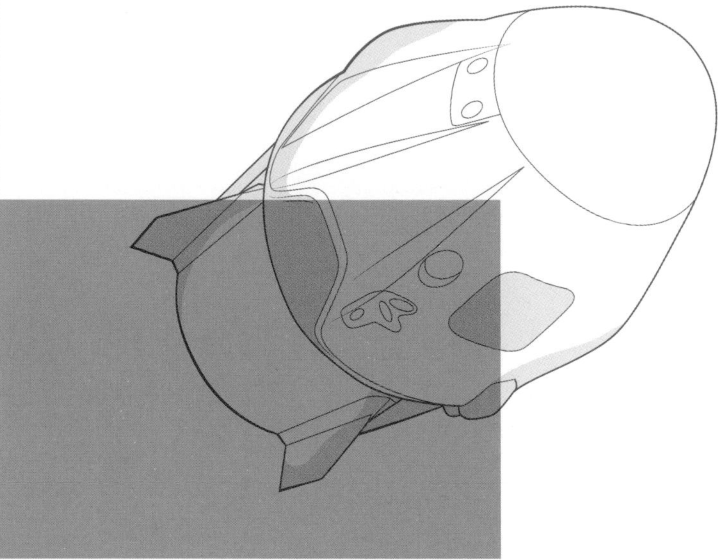

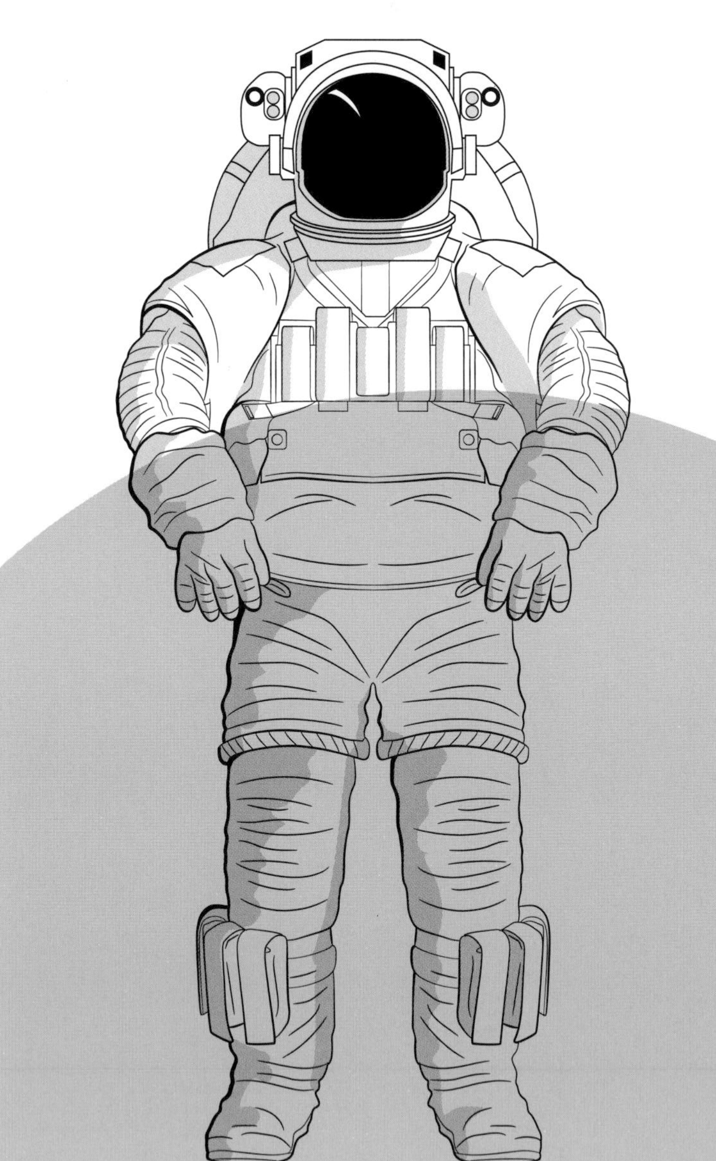

CONTENTS

1

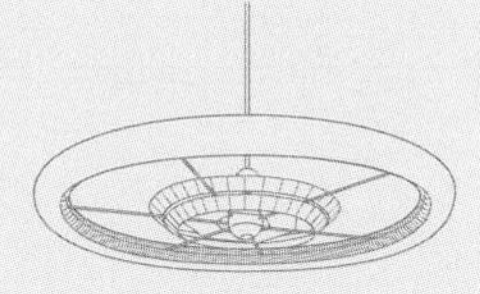

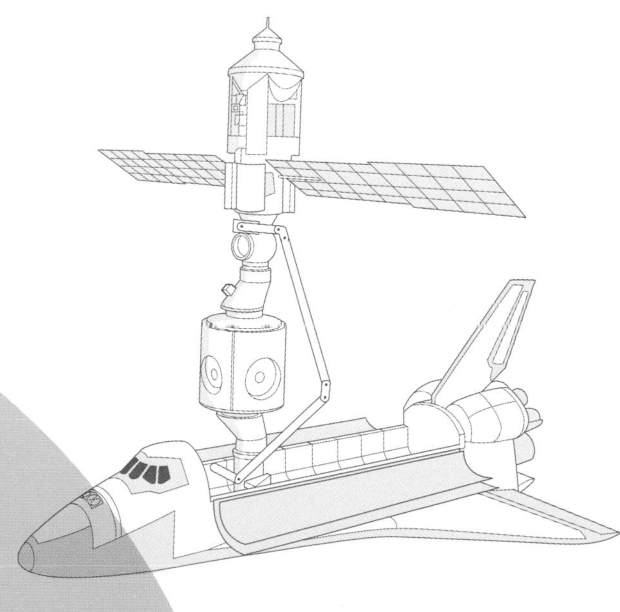

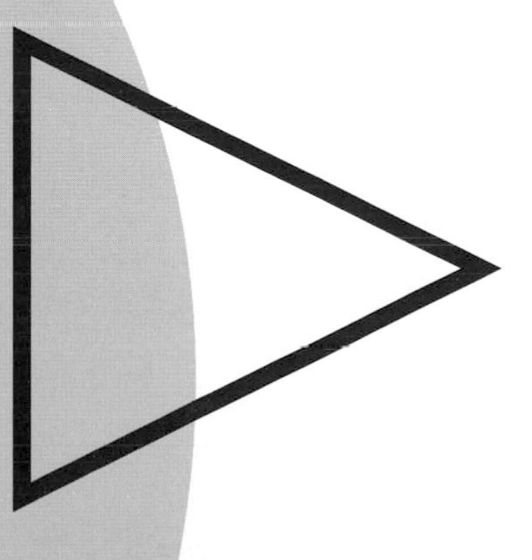

2

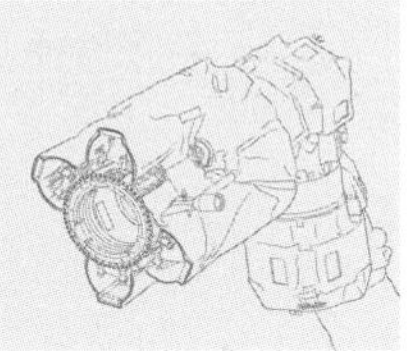

3

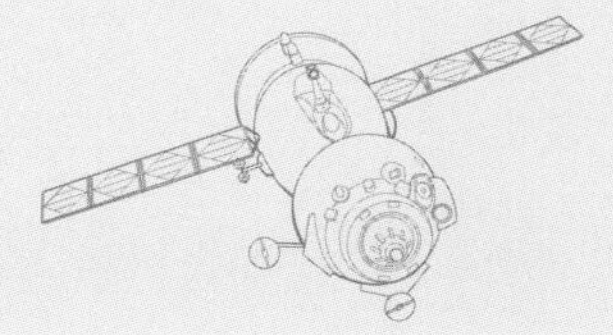

4

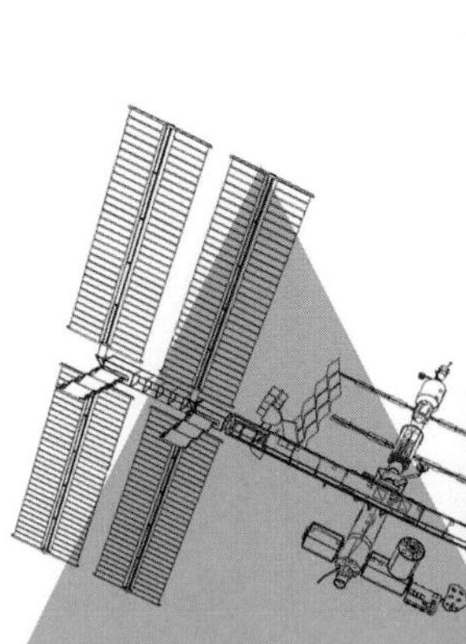

5

6

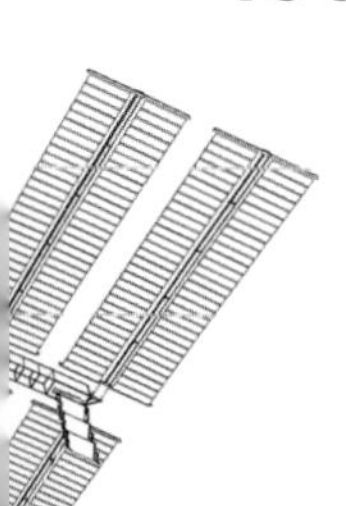

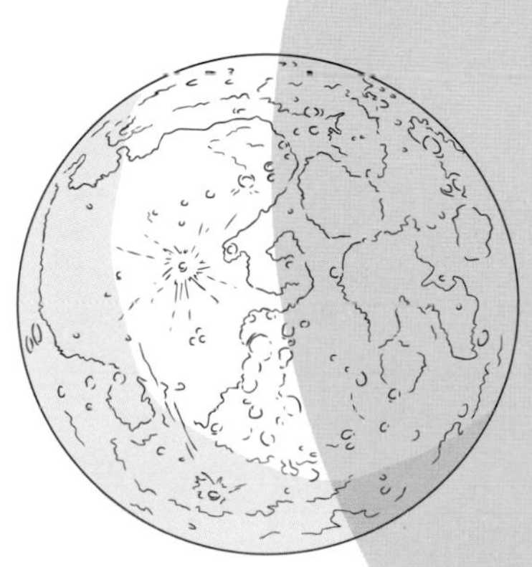

AT HOME IN SPACE

Long before the first astronaut crews launched in the 1960s, pioneering thinkers realized a station orbiting Earth, less than a few hundred miles up, would provide us with a unique resource. It could be a base for observing both Earth and space, a laboratory for performing experiments, and a departure point for reaching farther into the Solar System. The idea of a space habitat where humans could live and work became a reality in 1971, when Russia launched the first space station, Salyut 1. Since then, scientists and engineers have designed and built increasingly ambitious and complex space stations, but currently just two exist. Today, Earth is orbited by the International Space Station (ISS) and China's Tiangong space station, although some national governments and private companies are planning to build more.

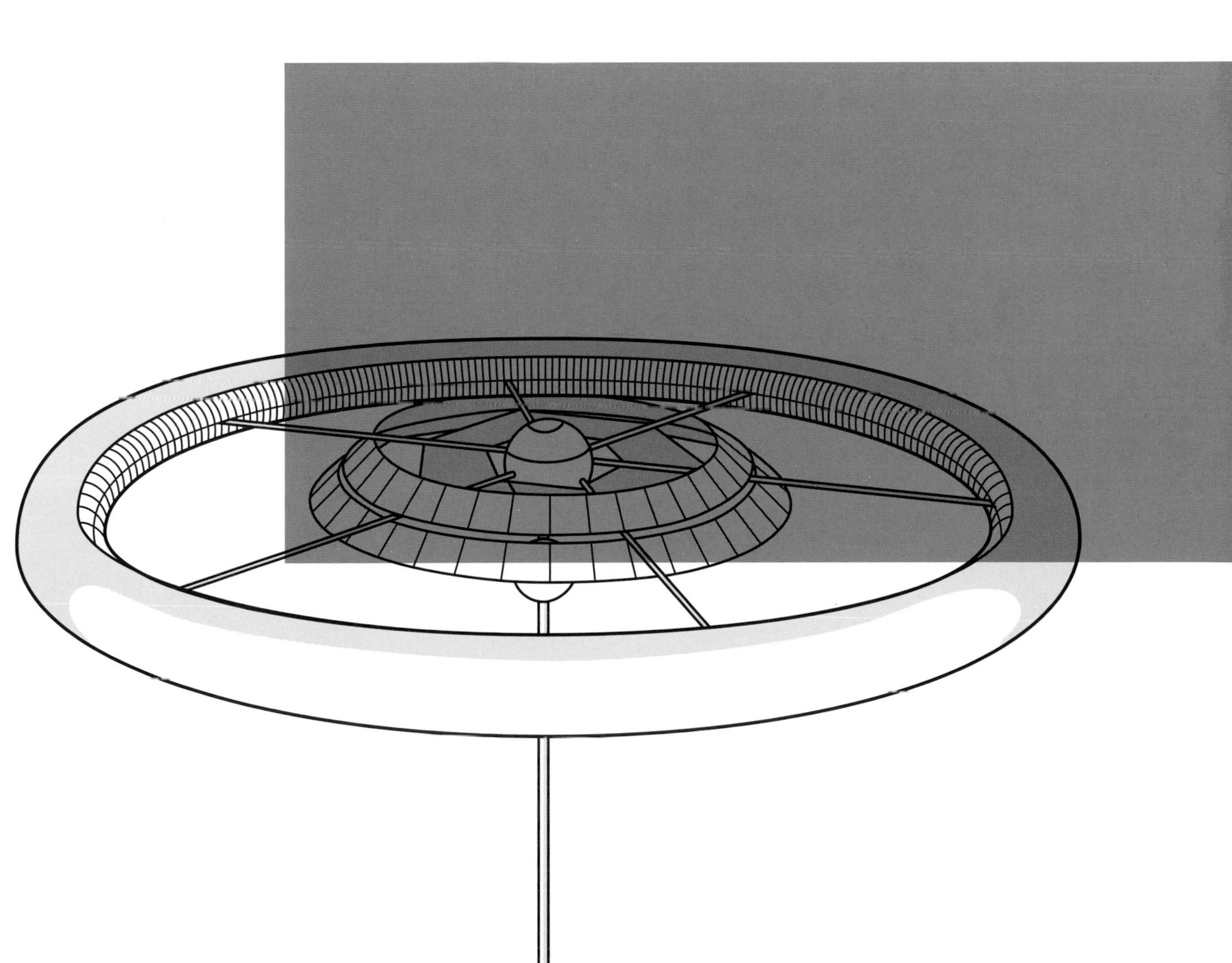

WHAT IS A SPACE STATION?

A space station is a long-term base in space, where astronauts take turns living and working. Space stations offer a unique environment for doing science, as microgravity makes it possible to perform exciting experiments that can't be done on Earth. There are currently two space stations in orbit: the International Space Station (ISS), built by multiple countries, and China's Tiangong space station.

DID YOU KNOW?

It has cost more than $100 billion to build and maintain the ISS.

▼ Team effort

During the 1950s and 1960s, the Space Race saw the US and the Soviet Union (now Russia) compete to become the dominant superpower in space. Over time, this competition developed into cooperation. Since 1998, the former rivals have worked together closely, along with other nations, to build and look after the ISS. The station is visited by astronauts from the US, Russia, and many other countries.

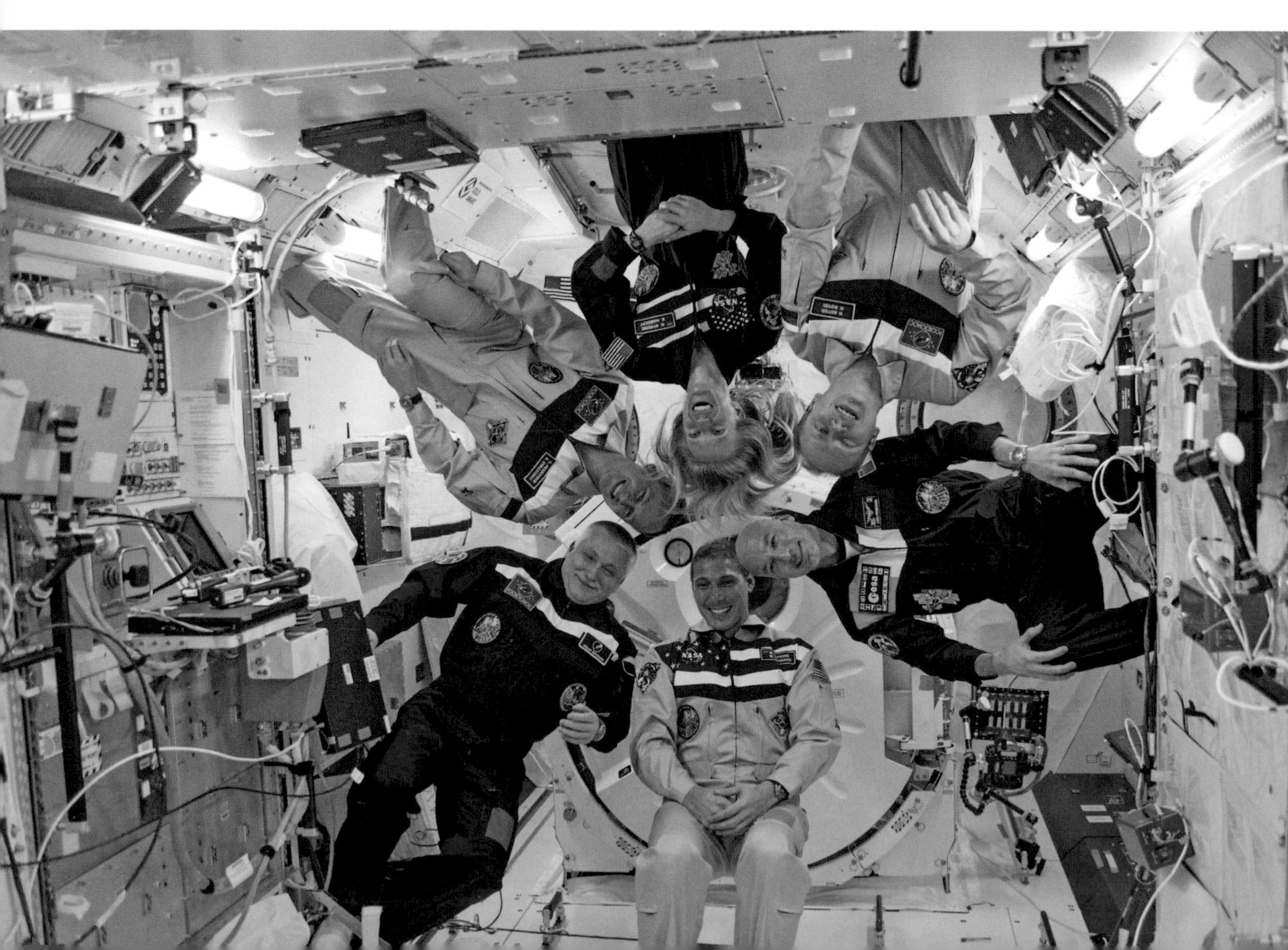

How does a space station stay up?

A space station stays above Earth because it's in orbit, a curved path around the planet made possible by its constant high speed. Any moving object in a vacuum (an empty space) will keep traveling in a straight line unless another force acts upon it. In the case of an orbiting space station, Earth's strong gravity bends this straight-line path into a constant free fall around the planet.

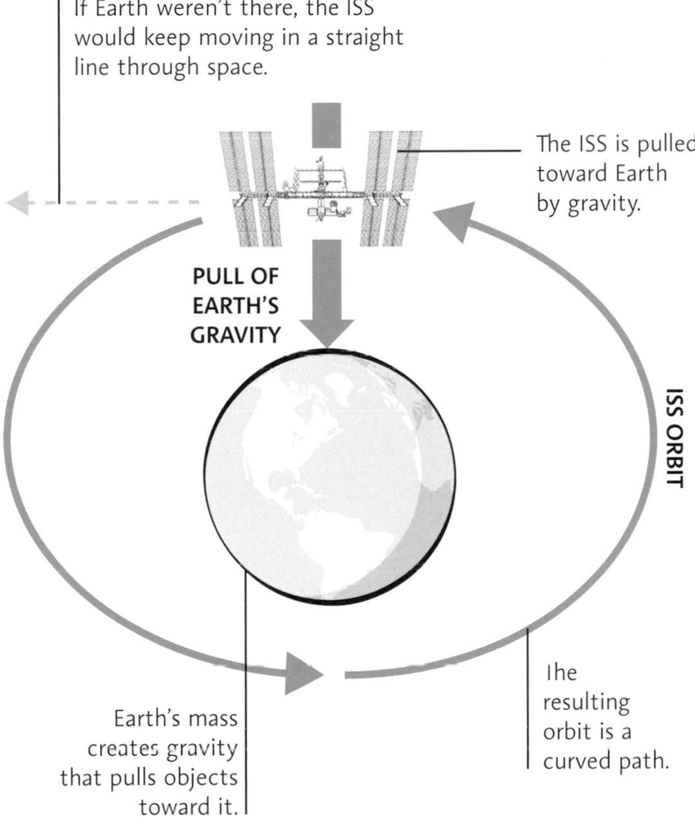

Life in microgravity

Using the phrase "zero gravity" to describe the conditions on a spacecraft is inaccurate. In reality, astronauts experience almost the same pull of gravity as we do on Earth's surface. Objects on the ISS don't fall "downward," however, because they're all together at the same rate on the path around Earth. Scientists call this floating effect "microgravity." It can be fun, but sometimes frustrating, for astronauts on board.

Extreme conditions

For astronauts, space travel is the ultimate challenge. Whether inside the space station or outside on a spacewalk, working in space tests their physical and mental abilities to the limit. They face many potential dangers, from exposure to harmful levels of radiation to the risk of being hit by space debris.

THE INTERNATIONAL SPACE STATION (ISS)

You don't need a telescope to see the ISS—it's bright enough to see clearly in the night sky with just the naked eye. This long-exposure photograph shows it passing over Wales, UK. You can find out when the ISS is flying over where you live by looking on NASA's "Spot the Station" website or on tracking apps available on a smartphone.

The Brick Moon

US writer Edward Everett Hale's 1869 story *The Brick Moon* describes the first fictional space station—a satellite that is accidentally launched with people onboard.

Wheel in orbit

In 1952, German-born rocket engineer Wernher von Braun, who later designed NASA's *Saturn V* (Moon rocket) in the US, described a wheel-shaped space station that spun to simulate the effects of gravity.

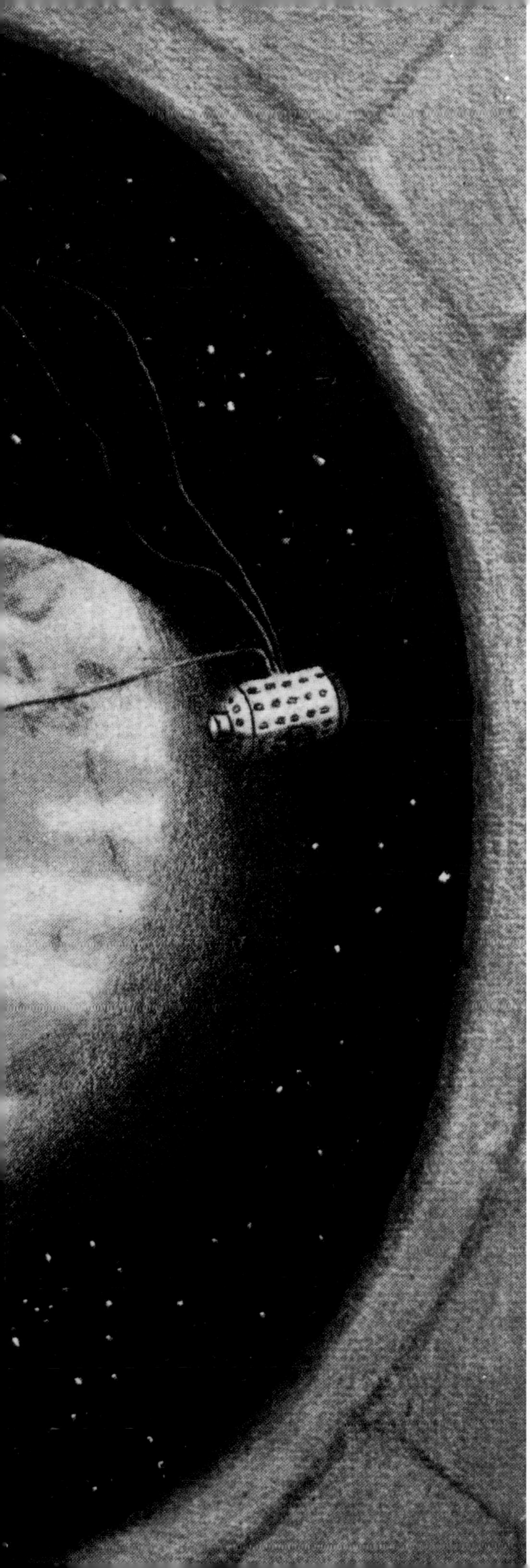

SPACE DREAMS

People have been fascinated by the idea of living in space for hundreds of years, but it wasn't until the 20th century that forward-thinking scientists and engineers began to develop rocket technology that could make those dreams a reality. Some of these visionaries realized that a base in orbit where humans could live would help us explore space and discover more about Earth too.

◀ Early idea

Austrian rocket engineer Herman Potočnik, also known as Herman Noordung, created the first detailed drawing of a potential space station with three parts and published it in 1929. The largest part was a 100 ft (30 m) spinning "habitat wheel" (lower left)—cables linked this wheel to a workshop module (top center) and an observatory (right).

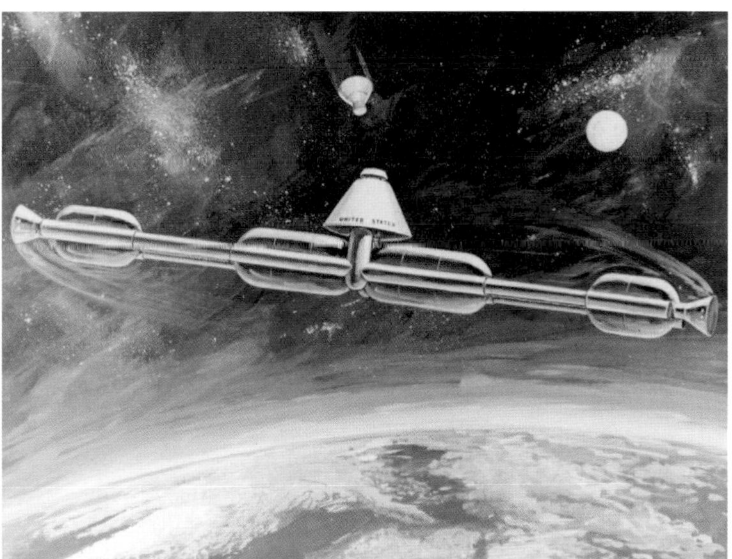

Spinning station

In the early days of human space flight, scientists weren't sure if people could survive in weightless conditions. By the late 1960s, many designs for a space station—like this one from NASA—used rotation to create a force that would mimic the effects of gravity. It was only with later space missions that scientists realized a space station didn't need to spin—living in microgravity was possible.

CITY IN SPACE

In the 1970s, engineers came up with designs for building huge, self-supporting space habitats. Nothing this ambitious has ever been built, but the most iconic design was the Stanford Torus. It consisted of a 1 mile (1.6 km) wide doughnut-shaped ring constructed using materials mined from the Moon or asteroids. Accommodating up to 10,000 people, the Stanford Torus would rotate once per minute, creating a force that mimicked the effects of gravity. Huge mirrors inside the ring would reflect light from the Sun onto the inhabitants.

Recreating nature

To reduce the need for supplies from Earth, the Stanford Torus would have its own "natural" environment, just like our planet, with plants and animals as well as water and air to support life. Perhaps one day, such enormous space habitats will become a reality.

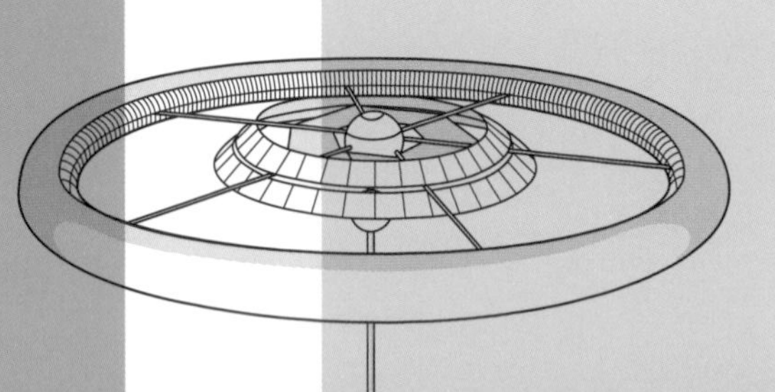

SPACE STATION HISTORY

The very first space station, Salyut 1, was launched in 1971, just 10 years after Russian cosmonaut Yuri Gagarin became the first person to reach space. The lessons learned while designing and operating Salyut 1 and its successors allowed scientists and engineers to keep creating ever bigger and better space habitats. The ISS, orbiting Earth today, is one of humanity's greatest scientific and engineering achievements.

MODEL OF SALYUT 1

SALYUT 1

1971

Launched by Russia, the first space station was shaped like a cylinder, with solar panels and a docking port for the Soyuz spacecraft. It remained in orbit for 175 days.

INTERIOR OF SALYUT 1 SPACE STATION

Salyut 7 had three main solar panels—extra panels could be attached to their sides.

SALYUT 7

1982-86

The last of the Russian Salyut space stations, Salyut 7 hosted six resident crews and four visiting missions before it was abandoned after a power failure.

SALYUT 7 (TOP) DOCKED TO SOYUZ SPACECRAFT (BOTTOM)

MIR

1986-96

Russia's Mir was the first large station to be built piece-by-piece in space. It hosted several Russian-led missions and visits from US space shuttles.

MIR-SPACE SHUTTLE PROGRAM PATCH

SKYLAB

1973-74

In May 1973, the first US space station, Skylab, was launched. Although the station was damaged during lift-off, three separate crews were still able to visit it, with missions lasting 28, 59, and 84 days.

Nearly 300

The number of experiments completed on board Skylab.

APOLLO-SOYUZ

1975

Marking the first international collaboration in space, the Apollo-Soyuz mission involved docking a US Apollo module with a Russian Soyuz spacecraft for almost two days in Earth's orbit. Three US astronauts and two Russian cosmonauts tested technology for docking spacecraft together.

MISSION PATCH OF THE APOLLO-SOYUZ PROGRAM

A specially designed docking module allowed crews to move between the US Apollo module (left) and the Russian Soyuz spacecraft (right).

APOLLO-SOYUZ TEST PROJECT

INTERNATIONAL SPACE STATION (ISS)

1998-PRESENT

The largest human-made structure in space, the International Space Station (ISS) was developed by 16 countries. Its first modules were launched in 1998, and the first residents reached it in 2000.

5

The number of space agencies that look after the International Space Station.

PATCH OF THE FINAL MISSION TO TIANGONG-1

TIANGONG-1

2011-16

The name of China's first space station means "Celestial Palace." It was visited by two crews aboard *Shenzhou* spacecraft in 2012 and 2013, including China's first female taikonauts (Chinese astronauts)—Liu Yang and Wang Yaping.

BUILDING A SPACE STATION

The earliest space stations were simple cylinder-shaped structures, which were sent into low Earth orbit in one launch. Later space stations, like Mir and the ISS, were constructed in stages. Self-contained units, known as modules, were launched into space one by one. They were joined together in orbit by astronauts during spacewalks and by using the space shuttle's robotic arm Canadarm1. The ISS is the most ambitious construction project in human history, involving dozens of rocket launches, space shuttle flights, and spacewalks to assemble it.

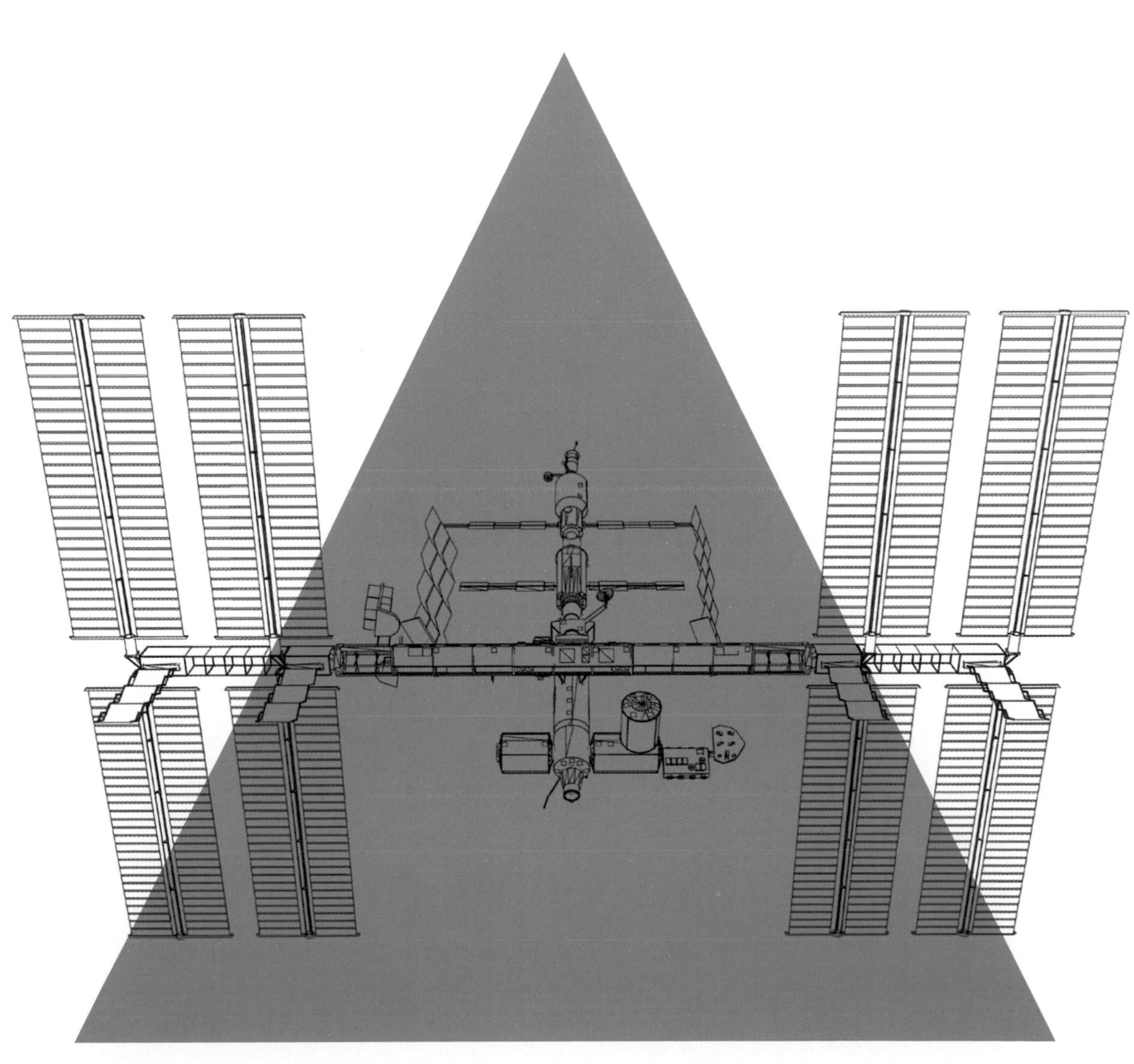

THE ISS EXPLAINED

Orbiting Earth about once every 93 minutes at a speed of about 17,500 mph (28,000 kph), the ISS is the largest and most complex object ever constructed in space. Astronauts carry out exciting scientific research there, which engineers and scientists on Earth use to develop humanity's spaceflight capabilities and improve life at home too. The ISS is kept running, safely and smoothly, by the space agencies of the US, Russia, Canada, Europe, and Japan.

▼ Home in space

The ISS is about the size of a soccer field and has as much living space as a six-bedroom house. It's made up of lots of cylinder-shaped units called modules, which link together, while a 356 ft (108.5 m) central "truss" acts as the station's backbone. Astronauts have been onboard continuously since 2000.

Map of the ISS

The first module of the ISS was launched in 1998. Since then, many more have been added, with the latest, *Nauka*, arriving in 2021. This color-coded diagram highlights some of the modules in which astronauts live and work.

KEY

- Columbus (ESA)
- Harmony (NASA)
- Kibo (JAXA)
- Nauka (Roscosmos)
- Unity (NASA)
- Zarya (Roscosmos)

Solar panels

Canadarm2 (CSA)

Cupola (observatory)

DID YOU KNOW?

The ISS orbits Earth 16 times in 24 hours, meaning the astronauts on board see 16 sunrises and 16 sunsets each day.

Space agencies

Five national space agencies are responsible for looking after the ISS. These agencies employ thousands of people around the world.

National Aeronautics and Space Administration (NASA), based in the US

Roscosmos, the national space agency of Russia

Canadian Space Agency (CSA), based in Canada

European Space Agency (ESA), formed by 22 countries, with locations across Europe

Japan Aerospace Exploration Agency (JAXA), based in Japan

INSIDE THE ISS

Every surface inside the ISS—the floors, walls, and ceilings—is in use, which can make the station a confusing place to navigate. There are signs on the walls to help astronauts find their way and handles to help them maneuver through the hatches between modules.

▼ Connected modules

Shown below is the US connecting module *Unity*, located between the US module *Tranquility* (right) and the Russian module *Zarya* (left). *Tranquility* contains gym equipment for the crew, while *Zarya*, the first ISS module in space, is now used primarily for storage. Mission patches stuck on the walls of *Unity* were left by previous crews.

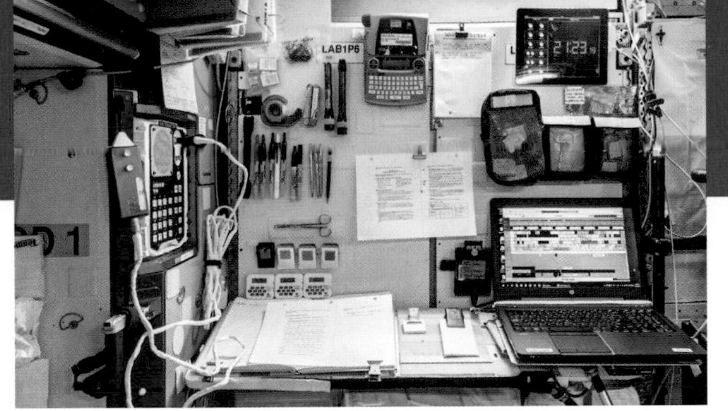

Tidy desk

An astronaut's desk is very different from a desk on Earth. You can put pens and papers anywhere: on the desk itself or on the wall or ceiling. Every item must be secured in place with Velcro, tape, or a clip to keep it from floating away.

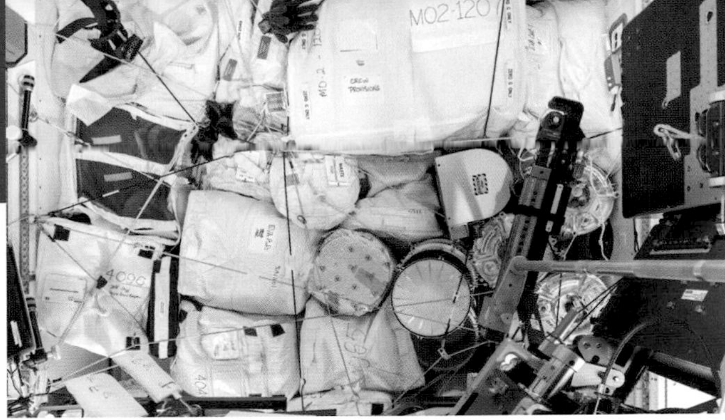

Storage space

Space is at a premium on the ISS, so every surface is designed to be used for storage. With so much stuff on board, from crew supplies to old garbage waiting to be sent home, it's essential to keep track of where things have been put so that nothing gets lost.

Zarya's external fuel tanks could hold more than 6.6 tons (6 metric tons) of fuel.

Radiators draw out heat to keep the module cool.

▲ Zarya and Unity

Zarya, meaning "dawn," was the first section of the ISS to go into space, on November 20, 1998. It flew solo until it was connected to *Unity*, launched two weeks later on the space shuttle *Endeavour*. The two modules were joined on December 6, 1998.

DID YOU KNOW?

Zarya is now used for storage, with other modules providing power.

Joining the modules

Connecting the modules was one of the most complicated maneuvers ever tackled in space. After chasing *Zarya* for two days, the crew used Canadarm1, a large robotic arm attached by one end to *Endeavour*, to capture the Russian module and gently pull it into place above *Unity*.

FIRST MODULES

The dream of constructing a joint international space project became reality when the first two modules of the ISS were connected in 1998. Built independently by the two major partners, Russia and the US, the two parts had different functions. *Zarya*, the Russian module, provided power and storage during assembly. The US-built *Unity* was used to connect future modules.

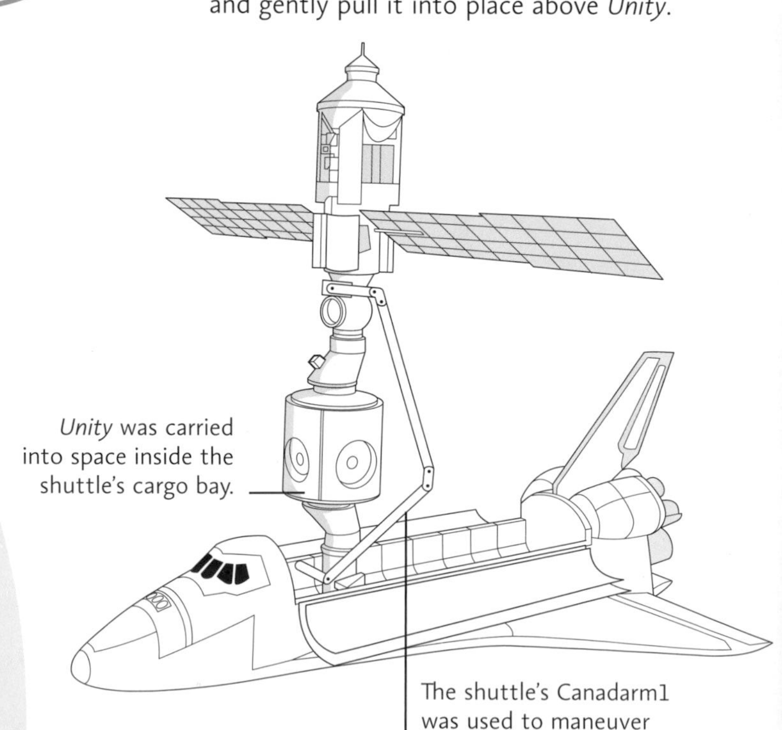

Unity was carried into space inside the shuttle's cargo bay.

The shuttle's Canadarm1 was used to maneuver *Zarya* into position.

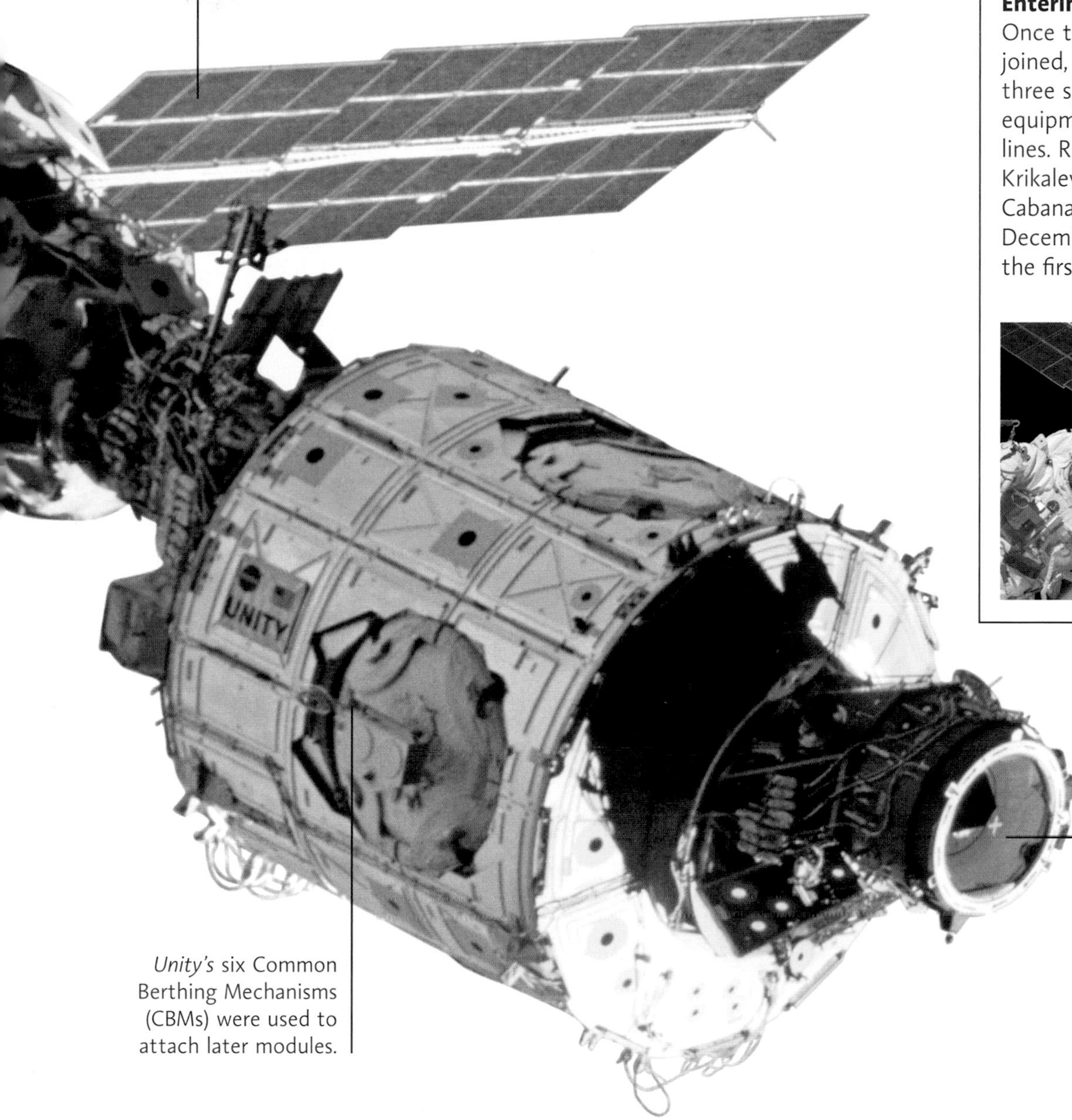

The two arrays (groups) of solar panels on *Zarya*'s wings provided power.

BIG MOMENT

Entering the ISS
Once the first modules were joined, astronauts carried out three spacewalks to install equipment and connect power lines. Russian cosmonaut Sergei Krikalev and US astronaut Bob Cabana opened *Unity*'s hatch on December 10, 1998, becoming the first people to enter the ISS.

Mating adapters on the CBMs allowed new modules to dock.

Unity's six Common Berthing Mechanisms (CBMs) were used to attach later modules.

Building Unity

Unity was built at NASA's Marshall Space Flight Center in Huntsville, Alabama. It is made up of more than 50,000 mechanical parts and has almost 6.2 miles (10 km) of electrical cabling.

International effort

The ISS is a collaboration between 16 different countries: the US, Russia, Japan, Canada, Brazil, and 11 European nations. Its success has shown that nations can work together for the benefit of humanity.

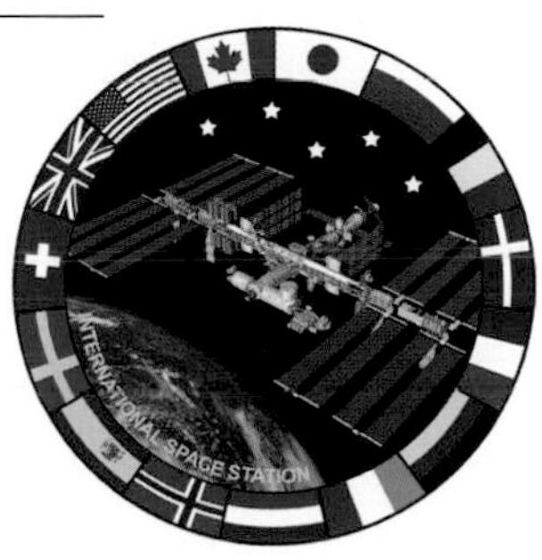

Space shuttle to ISS

The space shuttle consisted of three main sections: a pair of Solid Rocket Boosters (SRBs) that provided extra thrust on lift-off, the airplanelike orbiter that carried the cargo and crew, and the huge fuel tank. Only the boosters and orbiter could be reused.

1 The SRBs fired up along with the orbiter's main engines, lifting the space shuttle into the air. After two minutes, the SRBs separated from the orbiter, dropping into the Atlantic Ocean below.

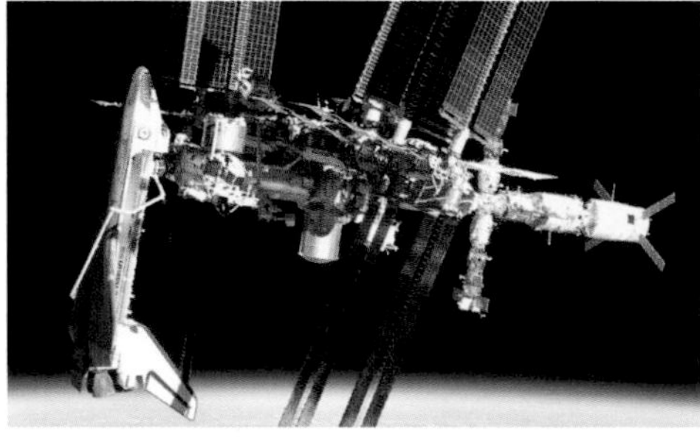

2 Once in space, a pilot had to skillfully dock the orbiter to the ISS. It could take a few hours to steer the spacecraft close enough to be docked.

3 When the orbiter reentered Earth's atmosphere, it glided down toward the runway like an airplane with its wheels lowered beneath it. A parachute opened at the back, which, along with the brakes, slowed the orbiter to a stop.

DID YOU KNOW?

The space shuttle fleet consisted of six orbiters: *Enterprise*, *Columbia*, *Challenger*, *Discovery*, *Atlantis*, and *Endeavour*.

THE SPACE SHUTTLE

The Space Transportation System (STS), better known as the space shuttle, was a reusable spacecraft that could carry huge payloads into space. It launched like a rocket and then, at the end of its mission, flew back down to land like an airplane. The first space shuttle flew in 1981, and until its retirement in 2011, it was the only NASA spacecraft that could transport astronauts into space. When construction began on the ISS in 1998, the space shuttle was used for transporting parts.

◀ Workhorse spacecraft

NASA built six space shuttles, all named after famous historical ships. Without the space shuttles, the ISS could not have been built. In total, the fleet completed 36 separate missions to transport ISS modules into space and assemble them as well as deliver supplies.

Cargo bay
The space shuttle had a huge cargo bay more than 59 ft (18 m) long. About 32 tons (29 metric tons) of cargo, equal in weight to five elephants, could fit inside.

Complex controls
The space shuttle was one of the most complex machines ever built and was very challenging to fly—it required specialist training of the best pilots.

BIG MOMENT

The *Columbia* disaster
In 2003, damage to the left wing of the *Columbia* space shuttle's orbiter caused it to break apart as it reentered Earth's atmosphere. Seven lives were lost in the tragedy, and shuttle flights were stopped for more than two years.

THE *COLUMBIA* CREW

ROBOTIC ARM

DID YOU KNOW?

Canadarm2 is the first robot to be able to repair itself in space.

Designed and built in Canada, Canadarm2 is the space station's highly advanced robotic arm. It was installed in 2001 and has since been used by astronauts to move large equipment, carry out maintenance, and capture visiting spacecraft. Canadarm2 is able to travel the full length of the ISS with the help of a mobile platform attached to the truss, the station's backbone.

Four cameras on the arm help the crew control its movement.

◀ Canadarm2

Just as cranes are used on construction sites to lift and carry heavy objects, Canadarm2 is used to move modules, cargo, and even astronauts from one part of the space station to another.

Long reach

Canadarm2 is 57.7 ft (17.6 m) long, which is about three times as tall as a giraffe. It has sensors that allow it to stop automatically if there's a chance of it colliding with another object.

The arm has seven motorized joints, so it can move with the dexterity of a human arm.

The "elbow" of the arm has one joint, while the "shoulder" has three.

Cosmic catch

Canadarm2 allows astronauts to capture uncrewed cargo spacecraft bringing supplies to the station from Earth. The arm is carefully attached to the spacecraft and slowly pulled in to dock the spacecraft with the space station. The crew can then open the hatch and see what they've been sent.

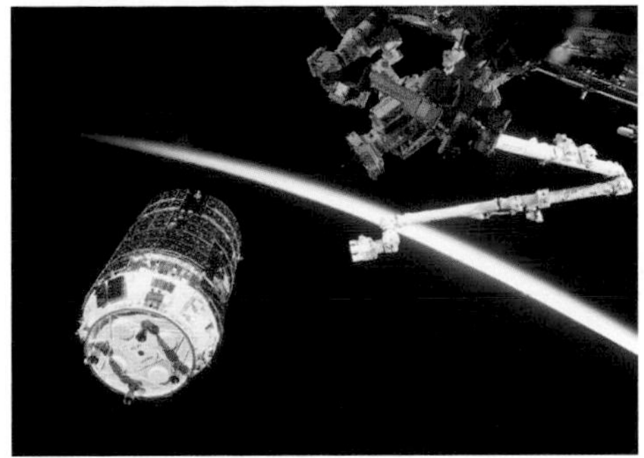

1 Watched by mission control and the onboard crew, the Kounotori cargo spacecraft slowly approaches the ISS by firing its thrusters. Once close enough, it gradually positions itself for docking.

2 Guided by the crew, Canadarm2 captures the spacecraft by connecting its gripping end (pictured below) to the docking port on the cargo spacecraft.

Gripping ends
Canadarm2 is not stuck in one place—it travels along the space station using the mobile platform. Astronauts can also move it around by connecting either of its two end onto a number of special docking ports and flipping it end-over-end, much like an inchworm.

The arm proudly showcases its home country's name.

Canada

The "wrist" of the arm has three joints.

Cupola control center

Canadarm2 can be controlled from two different places onboard the space station, one of which is located in the station's observatory module, the cupola (see pp.96–97). The cupola's six side windows and a large one at the top allow astronauts to watch Canadarm2 while moving it. Astronauts learn how to use Canadarm2 at the Robotics Training Center of the Canadian Space Agency.

OUT FOR A WALK

Sometimes astronauts have to step out of the ISS into the blackness of space, an activity known as a spacewalk, or Extra-Vehicular Activity (EVA). Occasionally, they have used Canadarm2 to help them travel from one part of the station to the other. Moving around the enormous ISS can be tiring, and astronauts can use the robotic arm to save them some time and a bit of effort.

Balancing act Anchored to the platform on Canadarm2, Swedish astronaut Christer Fuglesang installs a large ammonia tank, which is used to help keep the ISS cool.

Staying attached

Canadarm2 has a platform with feet restraints that secure an astronaut in position while it moves. A long ropelike cord made of steel, known as a tether, ensures that the astronaut is safely attached and can't float away.

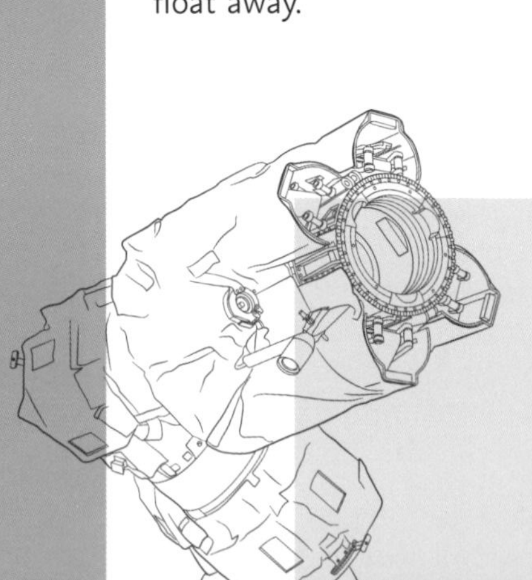

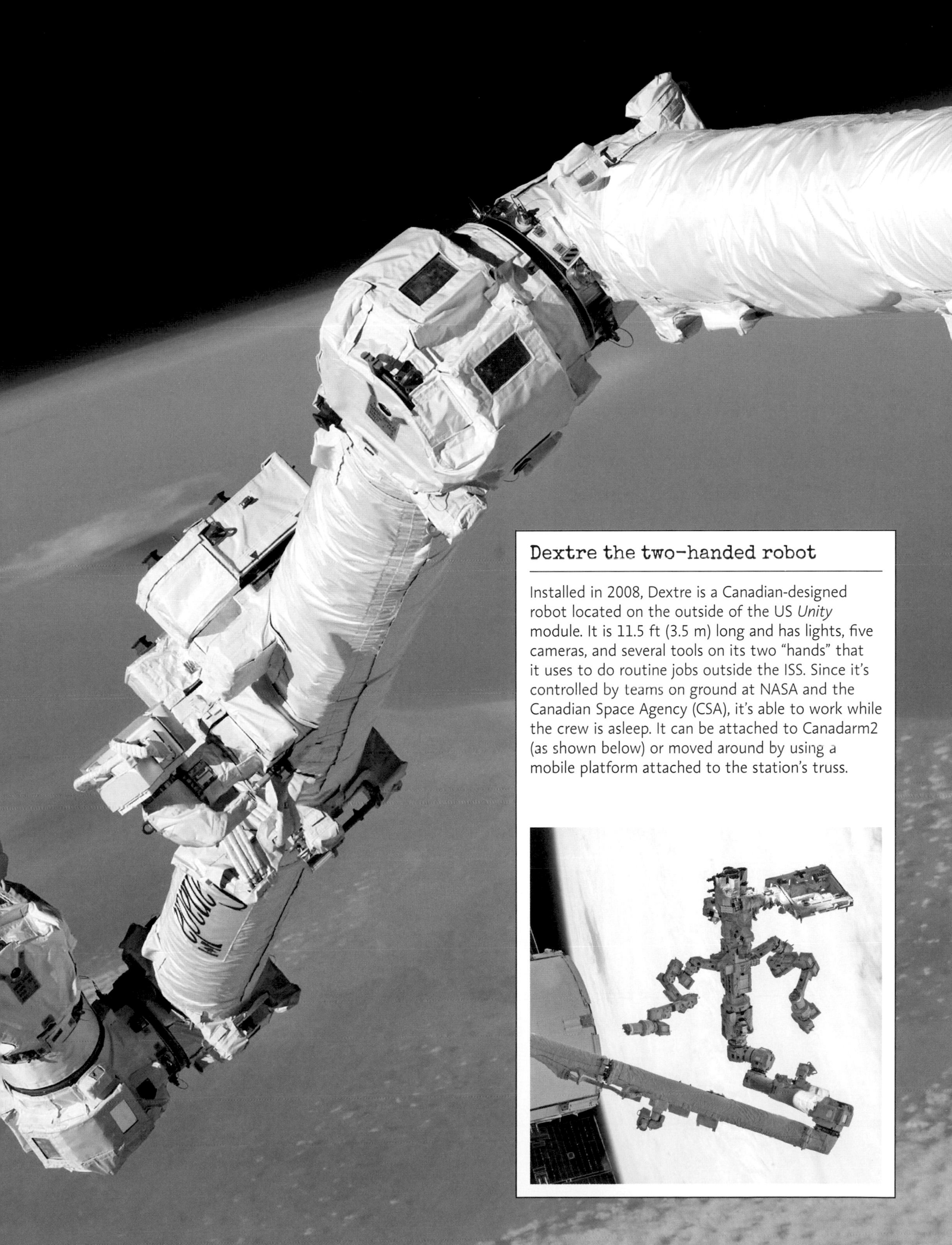

Dextre the two-handed robot

Installed in 2008, Dextre is a Canadian-designed robot located on the outside of the US *Unity* module. It is 11.5 ft (3.5 m) long and has lights, five cameras, and several tools on its two "hands" that it uses to do routine jobs outside the ISS. Since it's controlled by teams on ground at NASA and the Canadian Space Agency (CSA), it's able to work while the crew is asleep. It can be attached to Canadarm2 (as shown below) or moved around by using a mobile platform attached to the station's truss.

DID YOU KNOW?

Each of the solar panels is about 112 ft (35 m) long—that's nearly as long as three buses lined up back to front.

Essential power
Astronauts are completely dependent on the electricity produced by the solar panels to live and work on the ISS. Each panel functions independently, so if one breaks, the rest will keep supplying power.

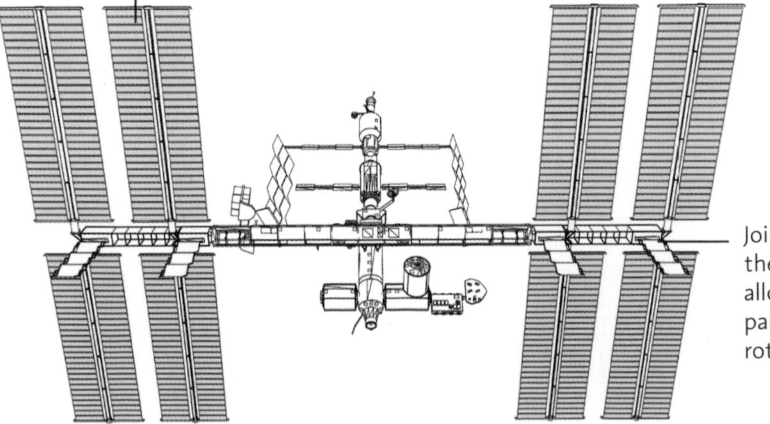

How it works

Covering each solar panel is an outer layer made up of solar cells (devices formed of the element silicon that convert light energy into electrical energy). Light energy from the Sun is absorbed by these cells and then passed to the solar panels' inner layers, where it is converted into electricity to charge the space station's batteries.

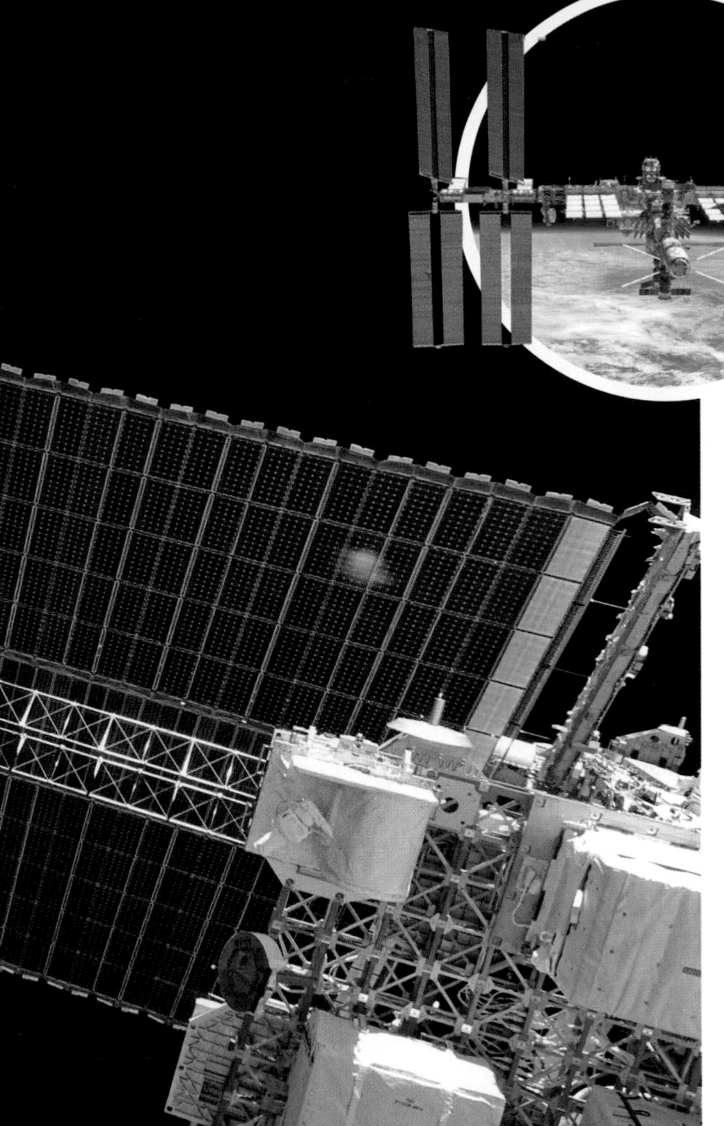

Giant "wings"
The ISS has 16 solar panels that are attached like wings to both ends of the truss (central spine).

SOLAR POWER

It's impossible for cables from Earth to supply electricity to the ISS, given that it orbits about 250 miles (400 km) up, so instead the station uses sunlight to generate power. It has huge solar panels that soak up energy from the Sun's rays and convert it into electricity. Some of the power generated charges up the station's batteries and is saved to be used when the ISS travels through Earth's shadow.

◀ Station powerhouse

Together, the solar panels on the ISS can produce up to 120 kilowatts of energy—enough to power more than 40 homes on Earth. It took several years and many spacewalks to add all of the solar panels.

New solar panels

With more modules and equipment being added to the space station, it's essential that there is enough electricity to power everything, so NASA is adding new solar panels to cover part of the older ones. Measuring 60 ft (18 m) in length, the new panels can be rolled up, which makes it easy for them to be loaded onto a rocket. The first of six new panels was installed in 2021.

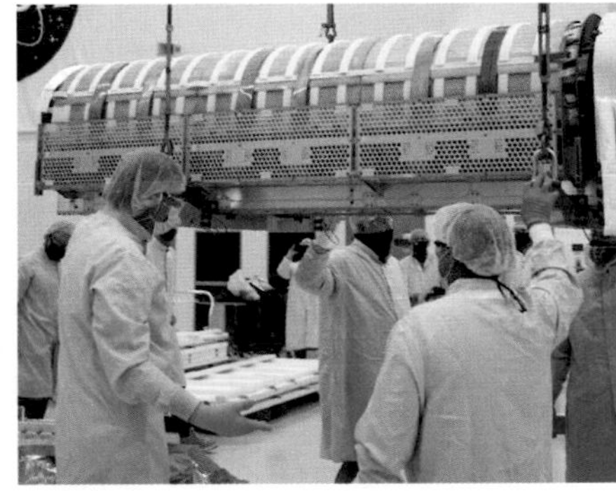

1 Workers at NASA's Kennedy Space Center, Florida, loaded the rolled solar panel onto a SpaceX Falcon 9 launch vehicle.

2 Astronauts conducted a spacewalk to position and attach the new solar panel. It was then carefully unrolled to its full length.

SPACE DEBRIS

The sky might seem clear when you look up, but there are millions of pieces of debris orbiting Earth. This debris is a mixture of things that humans have left in space: parts of rockets, tools dropped by astronauts during Extra-Vehicular Activities (EVAs), and old, out-of-use satellites. Over the years, some of these items have collided, generating more debris as a result. The debris is constantly monitored, and the ISS can be moved out of the way if there is danger of collision.

▶ Damage to Mir solar panel

Pieces of space debris whizzing around Earth travel at roughly 10 times the speed of a bullet fired from a gun. At such high speeds, even the tiniest object could cause damage if it crashed into the space station. When an uncrewed resupply vehicle collided with the Russian space station Mir in June 1997, it ripped a hole straight through Mir's solar panel.

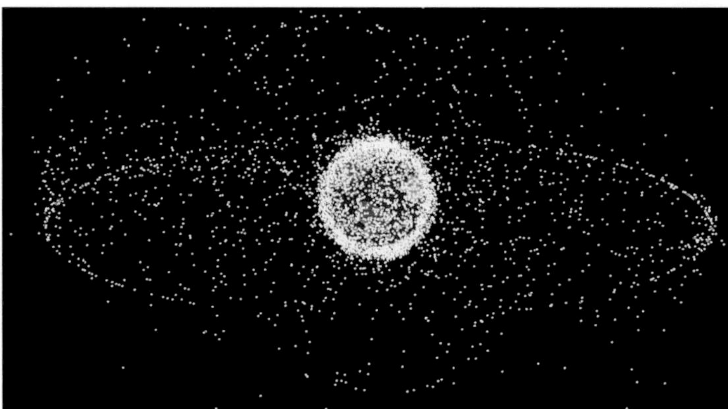

Space litter

This computer-generated image shows the larger pieces of debris scattered around Earth. The majority of them are in low Earth orbit, which stretches from 100 miles (160 km) to 620 miles (1,000 km) up. The US Space Surveillance Network tracks all pieces bigger than a marble.

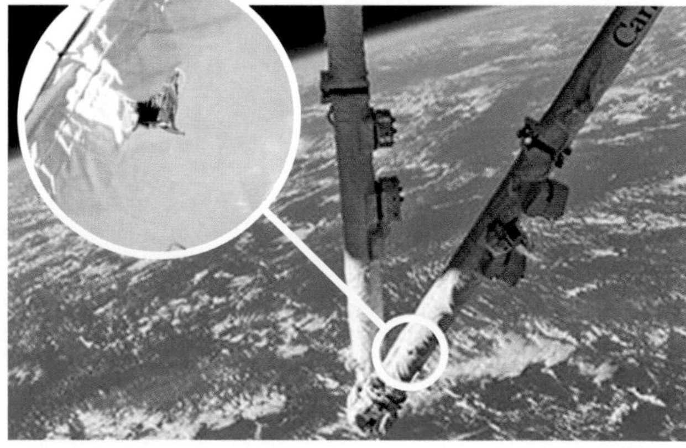

Canadarm2 damage

Although pieces of space debris are carefully monitored, the ISS can't avoid everything. On May 12, 2021, a tiny hole less than 0.25 in (about 5 mm) in size was spotted on its robotic arm, Canadarm2. The hole may have been caused by a fleck of paint.

Cleaning up

Space debris presents a serious challenge to space exploration. Each time pieces of space debris collide, more debris is produced, which causes more collisions, and so on. If humans don't start to clean up the mess, it may one day be impossible for a spacecraft to navigate safely through it. But scientists and engineers are working on solutions: new types of satellites that are able to capture space debris and destroy it.

Sling-Sat space sweeper
Sling-Sat is an idea for a spinning satellite that will catch bits of debris with its long arms and sweep them toward Earth to burn up in the atmosphere. It's being developed by researchers at Texas A&M University.

Space net
An experimental satellite called RemoveDEBRIS is being tested as a way to catch space debris. It will either capture pieces of debris in a net or grab the pieces and reel them in with a harpoon before taking them closer to Earth to burn up in the atmosphere.

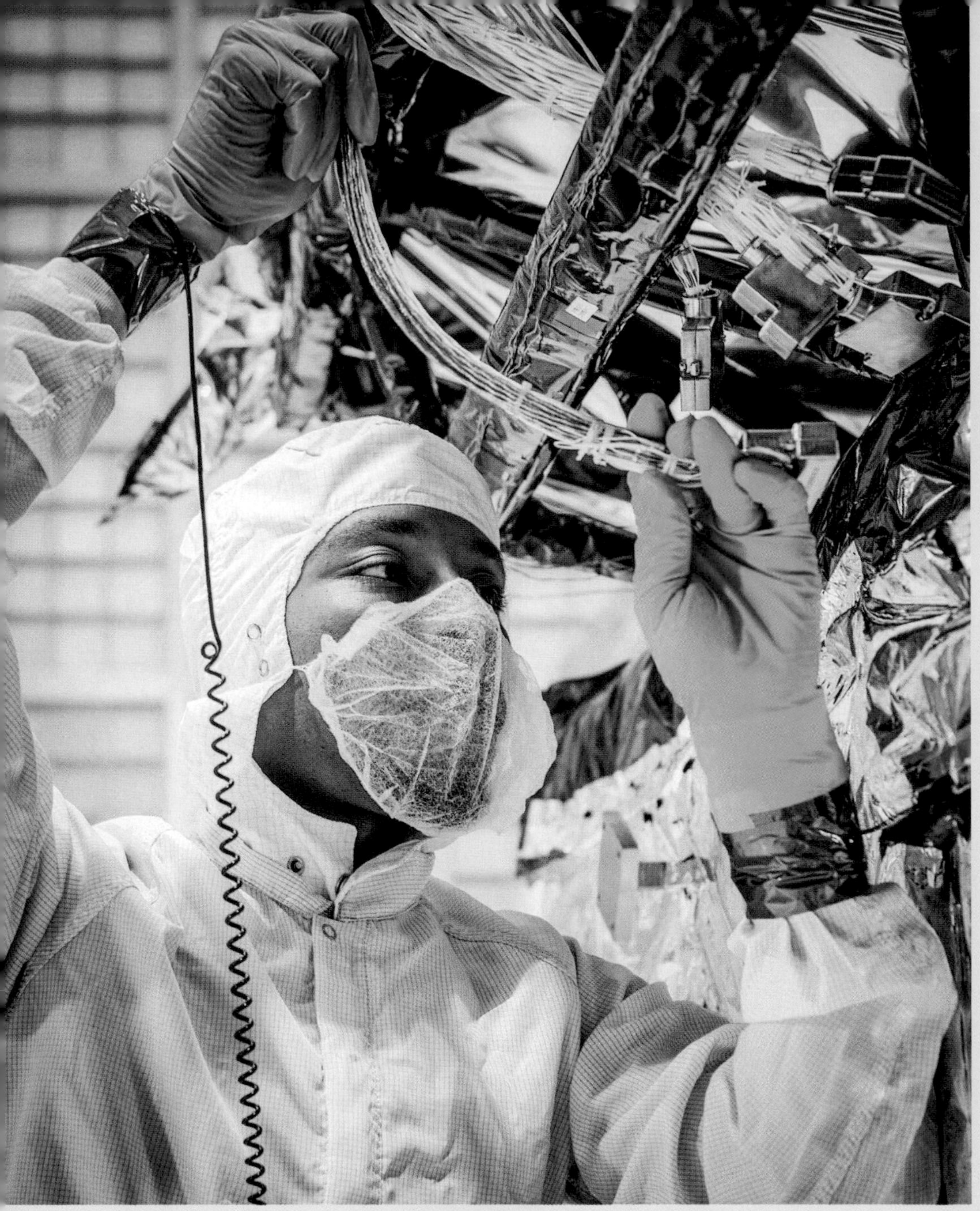

ROLES BEHIND THE SCENES

ENGINEER

Almost every piece of equipment sent into space was developed by an engineer, from gravity-defying rockets to toilets adapted for weightless conditions. Experts in math and science, engineers play an essential role in designing, building, and testing the technology required for humans to travel into space and live and work there. Along with scientists, they continue to find new ways to make life safer and more comfortable for the crew on the space station.

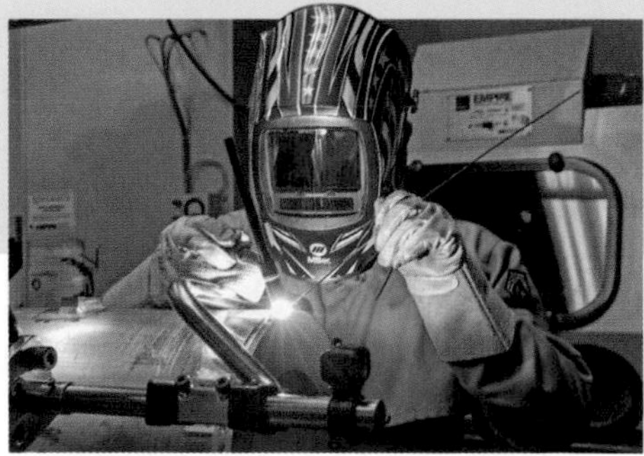

Time to test

Making a prototype (first version) of a piece of equipment they've designed allows engineers to test whether their invention works. Prototypes can also reveal problems that need to be solved before engineers finalize a design.

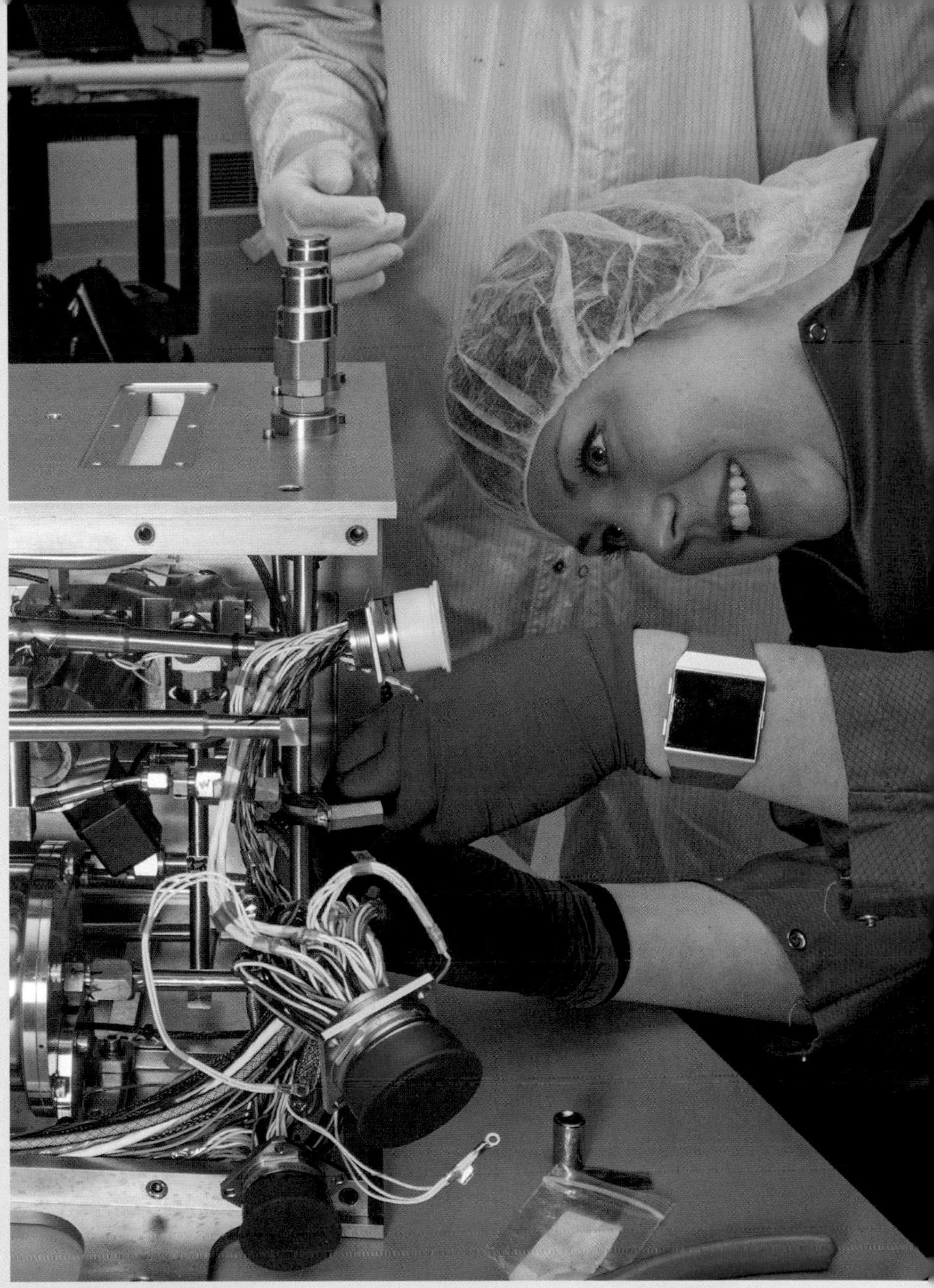

Final checks ▲

Engineers specialize in different fields, such as electronics, materials, or mechanics. They check that equipment works correctly and is safe to be used in space.

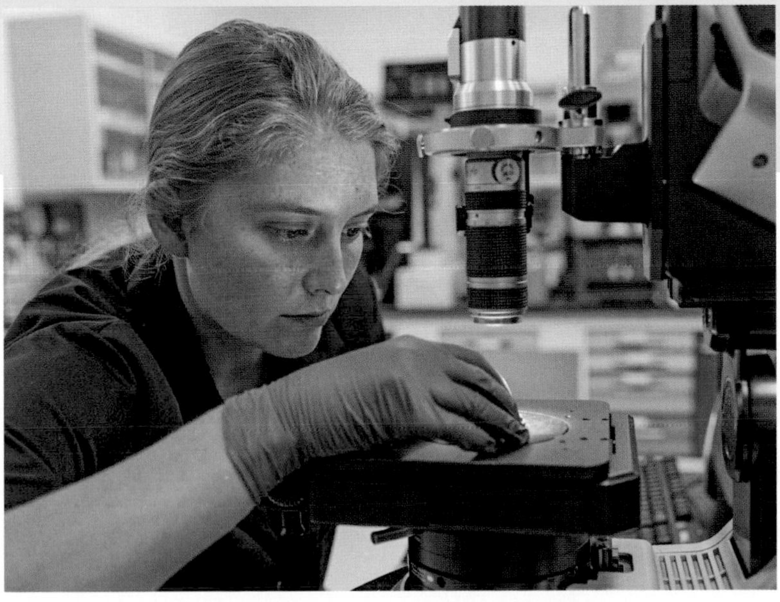

Lab analysis

Engineers are constantly trying to develop new materials that are strong enough to withstand the harsh conditions of space but light enough to be launched easily. Here, Liz Tomsik, an engineer in the Materials Analysis Lab at the Kennedy Space Center in Florida, examines a new material with a microscope.

BUILDING A MODULE

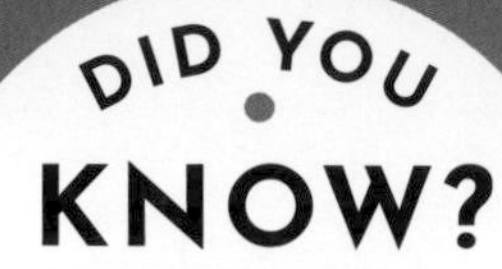

In July 2021, a new Multipurpose Laboratory Module (MLM), also known as *Nauka*, meaning "science" in Russian, was added to the space station. At just over 43 ft (13 m) long, *Nauka* is the largest Russian module ever built. Russian cosmonauts will use their new module to carry out experiments.

DID YOU KNOW?

Nauka's design is based on the space station's very first module, *Zarya*.

Check and check again Engineers had a long list of more than 750 separate checks they had to carry out before *Nauka* was approved for launch.

▼ Built on Earth

A number of tests on *Nauka* took place at the Baikonur Cosmodrome, Kazakhstan, in an exceptionally clean environment to prevent contamination by dirt or germs. Engineers wore overalls, masks, hats, and gloves at all times. There were multiple delays to the project—the module was supposed to launch in 2007, but it wasn't ready until 2021.

Nauka in space

Nauka (left) docked with the ISS, attaching to the Russian *Zvezda* module, on July 29, 2021. Its solar panels were opened, powering up the module. Shortly after, its thrusters fired by mistake, causing the ISS to rotate one-and-a-half times before mission control and the crew regained control!

Large radiator panels push heat from the module out into space, preventing it from getting too hot.

During construction, yellow stairs and platforms were put up to let engineers safely access every part of the module.

CHINA GOES TO SPACE

In 2003, China sent its first crewed spacecraft into orbit when taikonaut (Chinese astronaut) Yang Liwei flew a solo mission aboard the *Shenzhou 5* spacecraft. Since then, the country's space program has advanced rapidly, and China now rivals the US and Russia as a leading space power.

▶ Rocket launch

All China's crewed missions have blasted off from the Jiuquan Satellite Launch Center, Inner Mongolia, in the Gobi Desert. Its crewed spacecraft, named Shenzhou, are launched using the powerful two-stage Long March 2F rocket. *Shenzhou 10* (pictured) was used for the fifth crewed mission, launched in 2013.

Building a Shenzhou spacecraft

Shenzhou spacecraft resemble a supersized version of Russia's Soyuz. They are made up of a cylindrical orbital module at the top, a bell-shaped reentry module in the middle, and a cylinder-shaped service module at the base, which is equipped with solar panels.

Training taikonauts

China's taikonauts are selected from the military services and train at a center outside the capital, Beijing. Here, three taikonauts practice in a reentry capsule. Since 2015, Chinese and ESA astronauts have trained together to prepare for a joint mission to the Tiangong space station.

DID YOU KNOW?

The Long March 2F rocket is popularly known in China as *Shenjian*, which means "divine arrow."

Future taikonauts

China sees space exploration as a way to inspire the country's next generation of scientists and engineers. Taikonauts deliver lectures from orbit, and space scholarships and summer camps are available for students.

BIG MOMENT

First female taikonaut
Pilot Liu Yang became the first Chinese woman to enter space in 2012 as part of the three-person crew of the Shenzhou 9 mission. During her 13-day spaceflight, she performed experiments in space medicine.

Orbiting Earth

This illustration shows what Tiangong will look like in orbit when fully assembled. There are two lab modules—*Wentian* and *Mengtian*—attached to either side of the docking hub (left and right), a cargo spacecraft (Tianzhou, lower left), the *Tianhe* module in the center, and two visiting Shenzhou spacecraft (upper and lower center). The station is planned to be in use for 10 years.

TIANGONG SPACE STATION

Core module

The station's central module, *Tianhe*, has a control center and contains living quarters for the astronauts on board. It also provides power and has its own robotic arm, which will be used to link future modules to the station.

China's space stations are known by the name Tiangong, which means "Heavenly Palace." Tiangong-1 and Tiangong-2, launched in 2011 and 2016, were experimental stations designed to test techniques, such as docking in space. Their successor, known simply as "Tiangong space station" or just Tiangong, is a more complex station built (like the ISS) by assembling modules in orbit. The core module, *Tianhe*, was launched in 2021, and two more—both laboratory modules—will be added in 2022.

◀ Inside Tianhe

Tianhe ("Harmony of the Heavens") has living space for up to three taikonauts (Chinese astronauts), complete with exercise equipment, a communication center, and—most importantly—a life-support system. This photo, taken on the first crewed mission to Tiangong, Shenzhou 12, shows taikonaut Tang Hongbo inside the module while his colleague Nie Haisheng is out on a spacewalk.

BIG MOMENT

First crew

On June 17, 2021, Tiangong welcomed its first taikonauts. The Shenzhou 12 crew (from left to right, Tang Hongbo, commander Nie Haisheng, and Liu Boming) spent 90 days there—three times the length of any previous crewed Chinese space mission.

Return to Earth

After 92 days in orbit, during which the crew carried out various scientific experiments, the return capsule of Shenzhou 12 reentered the atmosphere and landed safely on Earth on September 17, 2021. Shenzhou 12's success paved the way for longer, more ambitious crewed missions to Tiangong.

PREPARE FOR LAUNCH

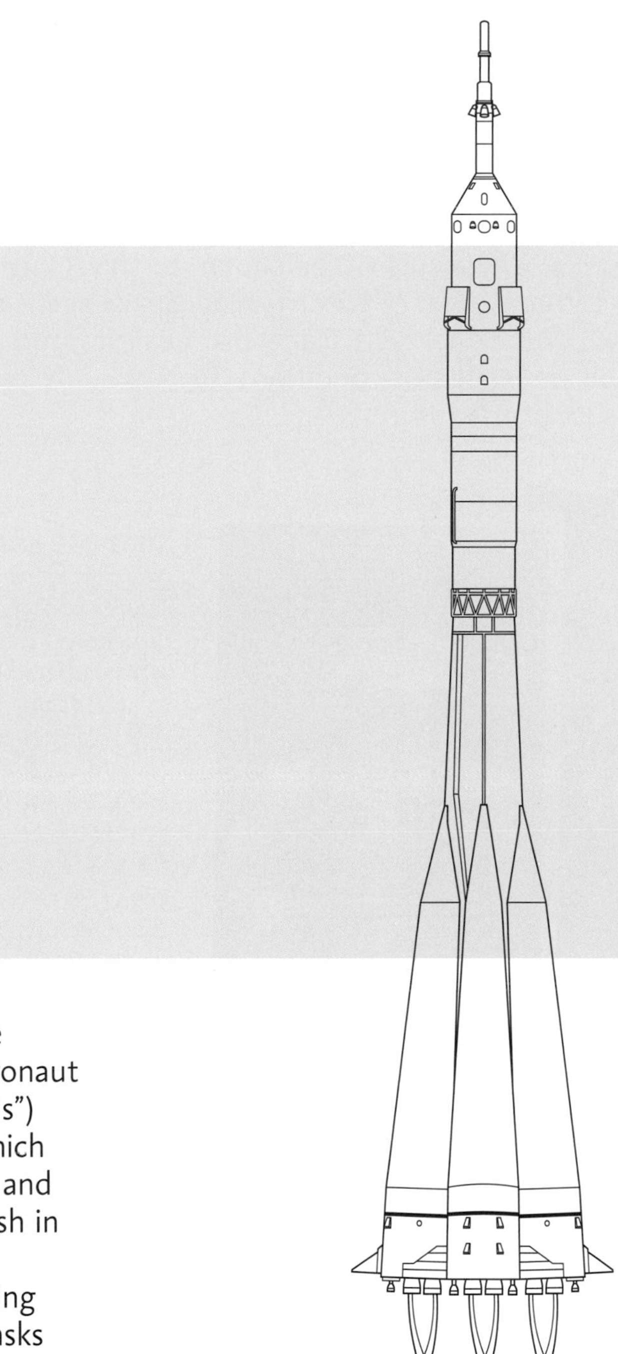

A journey into space starts long before launch day. Years before a mission, astronaut candidates (known at NASA as "ASCANs") begin a long training program during which they learn the skills they'll need to live and work safely in space—from how to wash in microgravity to making repairs during a spacewalk. There is no such thing as being too prepared if you're an astronaut. Tasks are practiced countless times on Earth to make sure that from the moment a spacecraft takes off, everyone on board knows exactly what they need to do. Finally, after years of training, when launch day arrives, it's a thrilling, bone-shaking ride up to low Earth orbit.

WHAT MAKES AN ASTRONAUT

People aren't born as astronauts. To be chosen to travel into space, you need to go through years of hard training. Space agencies look for candidates with technical skills, leadership qualities, and an ability to handle difficult or dangerous conditions. Then, they develop them into the astronauts of the future.

Recruitment posters

Before space agencies can choose candidates for astronaut training, they need to attract people to apply. With plans in place to put humans on the Moon again, and even one day on Mars, astronauts could be needed for all sorts of jobs—from explorers to farmers. Could these recruitment posters be the NASA advertisements of the future?

Routes in

Before being accepted for astronaut training, applicants first need to have several years of professional experience. There are a few different job roles that can lead to a possible career as an astronaut, such as pilot, scientist, or doctor.

Pilot
Highly experienced pilots are needed to fly spacecraft. They are sometimes selected from a pool of test pilots—people who fly new aircraft to check new designs.

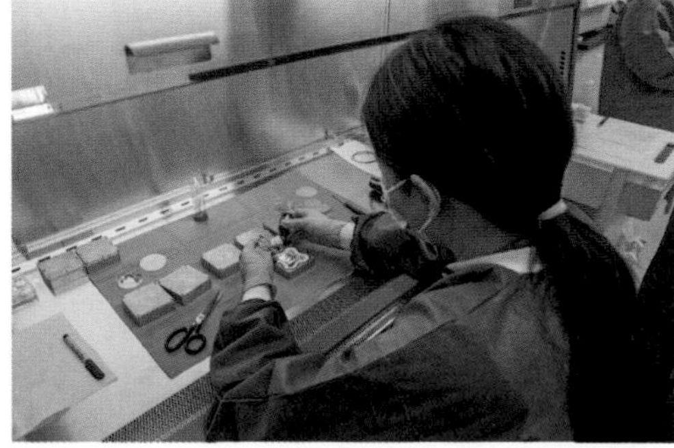

Scientist
Candidates are chosen from a wide range of scientific backgrounds. Qualifications can be in math, engineering, biology, physics, computer science, or medicine.

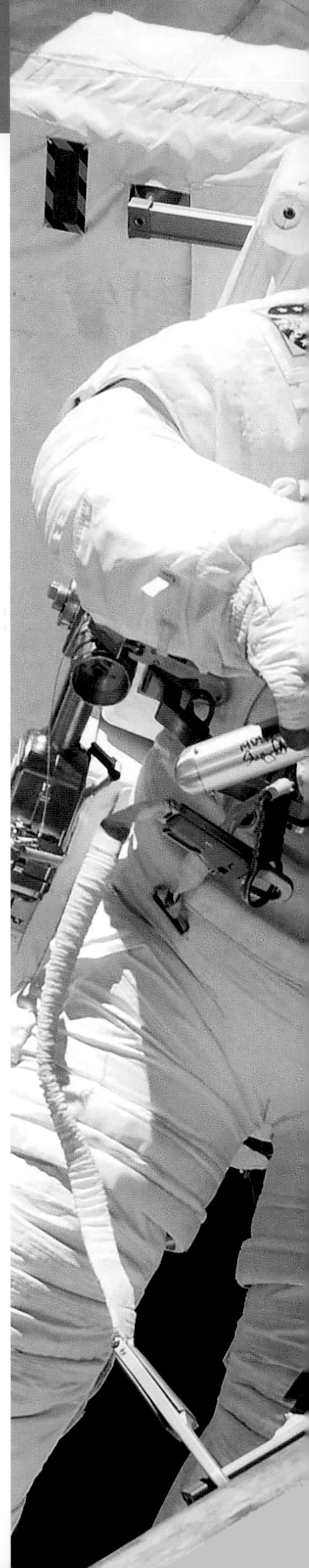

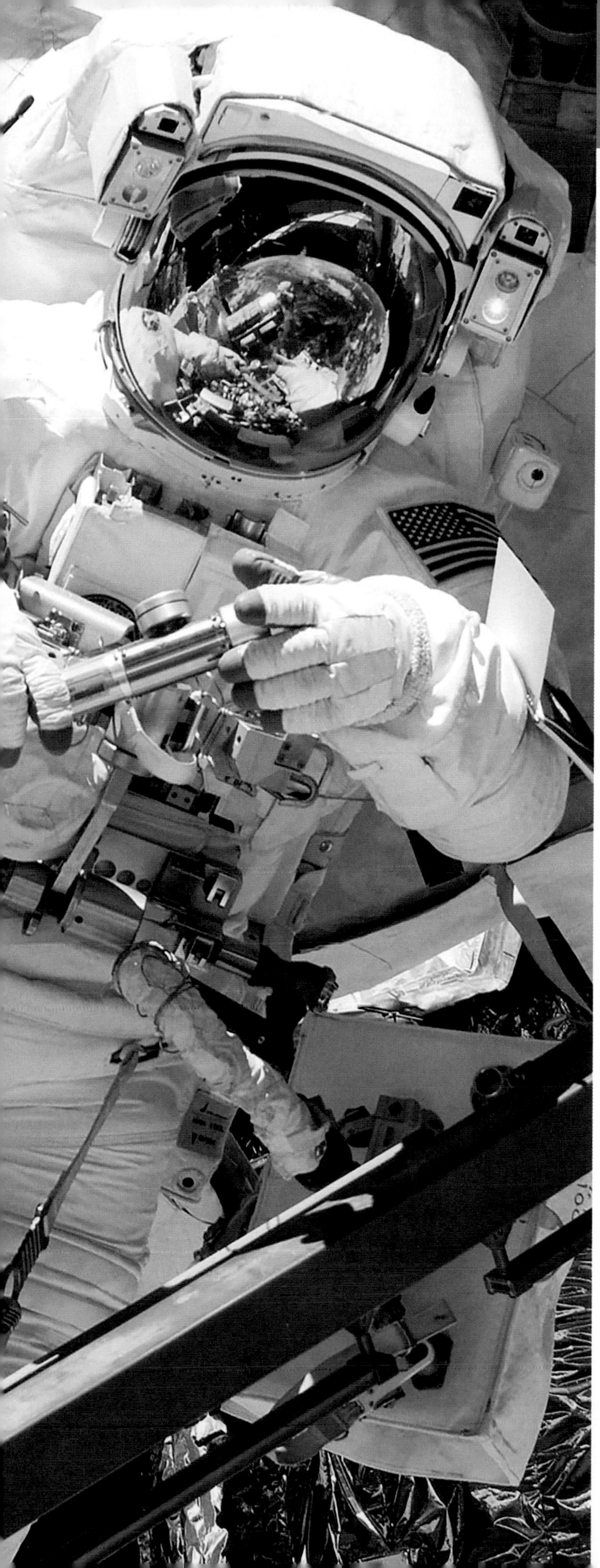

◀ Floating free

Going through astronaut selection, basic training, and specialized mission training takes years of dedication and is incredibly demanding. But for the exceptional few—like US astronaut Alvin Drew (pictured), who in 2011 became the 200th person to go on a spacewalk—the reward is unlike anything else they will experience in their lifetimes.

ASCAN training

Trainees selected by NASA to become astronauts (astronaut candidates, or "ASCANs" for short) go through a two-year basic training program. Above, ASCAN Jasmin Moghbeli studies engine maintenance on a T-38 supersonic jet aircraft as part of her training.

Learning Russian

Russia's importance as a partner on the ISS program means that learning the Russian language is essential for all non-Russian speakers. On the Soyuz, which is used to transport crews to the ISS, all launching and landing procedures are in Russian.

ROLES BEHIND THE SCENES

ASTRONAUT

The early astronauts of the 1960s were selected to fly in space because they were exceptional test pilots. Since then, the skills required for the job have changed dramatically, and today astronauts are just as likely to have come from a scientific or engineering background. The responsibilities of the role are varied—on Earth or in space, no two days are ever the same. Astronauts must be able to work with precision, enjoy being part of a team, and stay calm under pressure.

Astronaut pins

NASA awards special pins to astronauts. They receive a silver pin once they complete basic training, which can take two years after being selected. A gold pin is given to astronauts once they've been to space.

Scientists in space

The ISS is an exciting laboratory for experiments that are impossible to do on Earth. Scientists can apply to have their experiments carried out there by astronauts, who are often the hands and eyes for these scientists. On Earth, before their mission, astronauts practice the experiments they will do.

Space communicators

Space missions involve thousands of people, but astronauts are the public face of space agencies. They speak at events, visit schools, and use social media to inspire people to learn about space.

SPACE CAREERS

It takes an enormous team to make a space mission successful. The space industry employs thousands of people, all working to push the limits of space exploration. If you're excited by the idea of designing equipment destined for space or giving the go-ahead for launch in good weather, then a career in the space industry could be for you. There are plenty of fascinating roles to choose from, whatever your interests. So, aside from being an astronaut, which other jobs are available?

ENGINEERS AT WORK

Engineers in the space industry build and test space stations, satellites, spacecraft, and all the systems and equipment needed to operate them. Creative problem solvers, they are also experts in math and science and specialize in different areas, such as electronics or materials science.

20

The number of different types of engineers employed by NASA.

WEATHER PREDICTION

The ISS orbits in a layer of Earth's atmosphere called the thermosphere. Weather works differently there than it does on the ground —it's influenced by factors like radiation from the Sun. So, for a successful launch and landing, meteorologists (weather scientists) must accurately forecast the weather not only on Earth but also understand atmospheric conditions in Earth orbit. They use data from observatories and satellite images to create their forecasts.

SPACEFLIGHT SUPERVISION

Staff at launch centers and mission control constantly stay in touch with crews, monitor data from sensors on spacecraft and the space station, and keep track of mission progress. They also act as messengers, connecting astronauts in space with engineers and scientists working behind the scenes.

MEDICAL SUPPORT

Space travel is tough on the body, and astronauts can face health challenges, especially from weakened bones and muscles. Aerospace medicine experts develop exercises to keep astronauts strong during long missions and generally help them stay healthy.

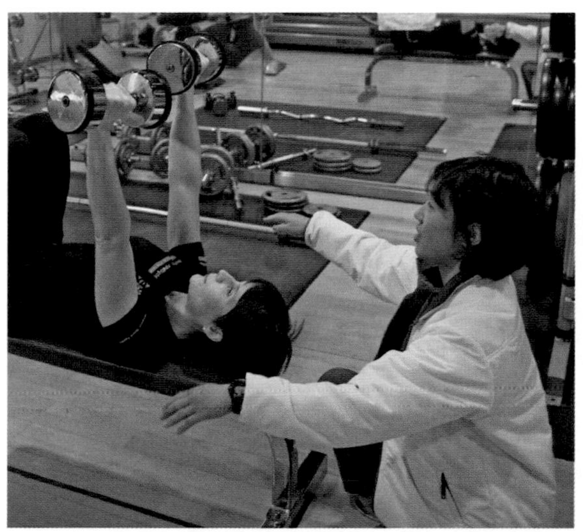

SCIENTISTS IN ACTION

Scientists use their knowledge and skills to discover new information. They prepare experiments, help astronauts carry them out in space, and study the results in order to solve problems and develop new technologies. Some scientists design equipment that will go into space, and a few even become astronauts themselves.

15

The number of different types of scientists employed by NASA.

PUBLIC AFFAIRS

With so many people curious about space and the work of astronauts, space agencies employ people to help explain to the public the details of rocket launches, new missions, and challenging spacewalks. Working in this area requires an understanding of the science behind the story and the ability to explain it to lots of people in a fun, exciting way.

OTHER EXCITING ROLES

▶ ELECTRICIANS

Electricity powers all activity in space. Specially trained electricians work for space agencies, designing equipment that works in extreme conditions.

▶ MISSION PLANNERS

The people who figure out the tasks to achieve the goals of a mission are called mission planners. They design schedules, plan crew training, and identify risks involved in a mission.

▶ ASTRONOMERS

Scientists who study planets, stars, and other objects in space are known as astronomers. They use huge telescopes on Earth and in space to make discoveries about the universe.

PRACTICE FIRST

The ISS and the spacecraft used to transport astronauts to it are some of the most complex machines ever built. Before stepping inside them, astronauts have to learn exactly how they work so that they can control them correctly and react safely to any problems that may occur. They train in life-size, exact replicas of the spacecraft, called simulators, on Earth and must pass several tests before they're allowed to fly for real.

▶ Simulator training

French astronaut Thomas Pesquet trained for his mission in a replica of the Soyuz spacecraft. A complex set of instructions written in the manual in front of him showed him how to operate the controls. The Soyuz is so cramped that astronauts often use a "poking stick" to tap hard-to-reach buttons.

Monitored on screen

Supervisors monitor astronauts during their simulator training sessions. To make sure that astronauts are well prepared, engineers program the simulator with unexpected technical glitches that the astronauts must resolve in order to pass their training.

DID YOU KNOW?

Astronauts train in simulators for at least 300 hours before their first mission.

GAGARIN COSMONAUT TRAINING CENTER

Soyuz replica
A Soyuz simulator is located at the Gagarin Cosmonaut Training Center (GCTC) in Star City, Russia. The center is a huge complex dedicated to spaceflight and training astronauts and cosmonauts. Star City is home to more than 6,000 people, many of whom work for Russia's space program.

GRAVITY TRAINING

Perhaps the most mind-boggling thing about space travel is microgravity—that things float, in contrast to Earth, where we're kept on the ground. The pull of Earth's gravity is almost as strong on the ISS as on the ground—it's what keeps the station orbiting our planet. But astronauts float because they, and the space station they live in, are constantly falling, or circling, around Earth. Without any ground to stop this fall, astronauts don't "feel" gravity like we do on Earth, meaning they can float. It can take astronauts time to adapt, but training on Earth can help.

▶ "Vomit comet"

To replicate microgravity on Earth is extremely challenging. The best way is a parabolic flight, when an airplane rises and falls repeatedly at high speeds causing its passengers to float freely. Parabolic flights are nicknamed the "Vomit comet," as they often make people feel sick.

Up and down

A parabolic flight is when a specially adapted plane climbs to a high altitude, then falls, much like a roller coaster. The plane doesn't have any seats for passengers and has padded walls to protect those on board against bumps. The plane is controlled by three pilots.

ZERO-G AIRPLANE

Ascent
The pilots increase power to the engines to make the plane climb upward. As the plane accelerates, the astronauts feel twice as heavy as they do on Earth.

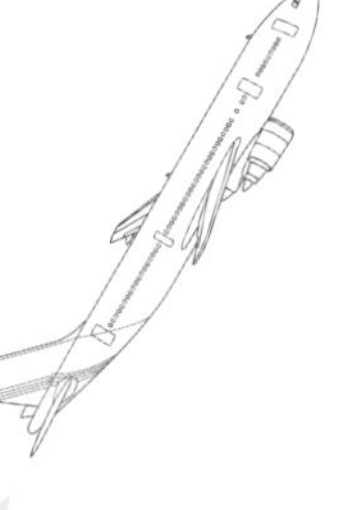

Parabola
At the top of the climb, the pilots slow down the plane. The astronauts float for about 25 seconds.

Descent
The pilots point the plane downward and take it out of the dive before it loses too much altitude. Once again, the astronauts feel twice as heavy as on Earth.

Once the plane has pulled out of one dive, the cycle starts again and can be repeated many times.

Astronauts at work

Parabolic flights aren't just for fun—they offer astronauts an opportunity to practice essential skills needed in space.

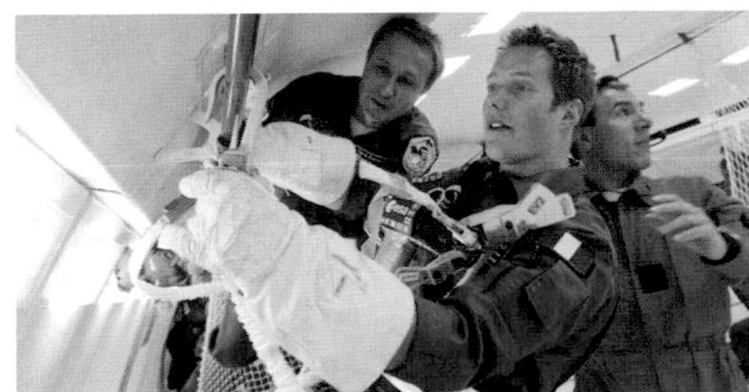

Mastering simple skills
Basic tasks like attaching and detaching safety tethers can be hard while seemingly weightless, but mastering these skills on a parabolic flight will help prevent an astronaut from floating away during a spacewalk.

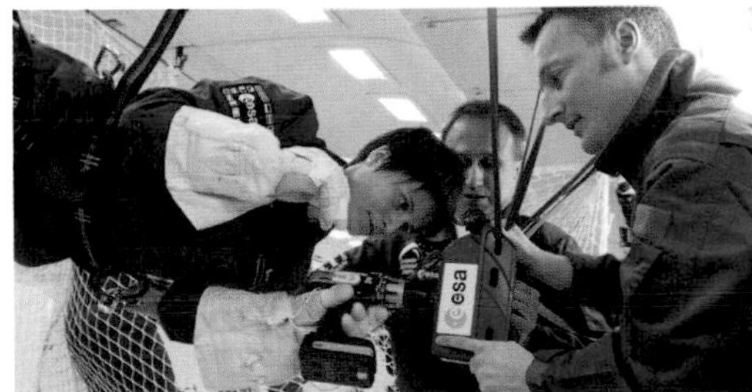

Power tool practice
Using a drill during a parabolic flight lets astronauts practice before their mission. Controlling power tools in space can be tricky, as they behave differently in microgravity.

Hypergravity

Astronauts aren't only exposed to microgravity during missions. They experience hypergravity too, when the force of gravity is greater than that on Earth's surface. To help them prepare, they train with a centrifuge, a machine that spins rapidly, subjecting objects inside it to strong forces similar to those experienced during launch and reentry.

Human centrifuge
An astronaut sits inside the capsule at the end of the arm. The arm spins, generating a force that pins them back against their seat.

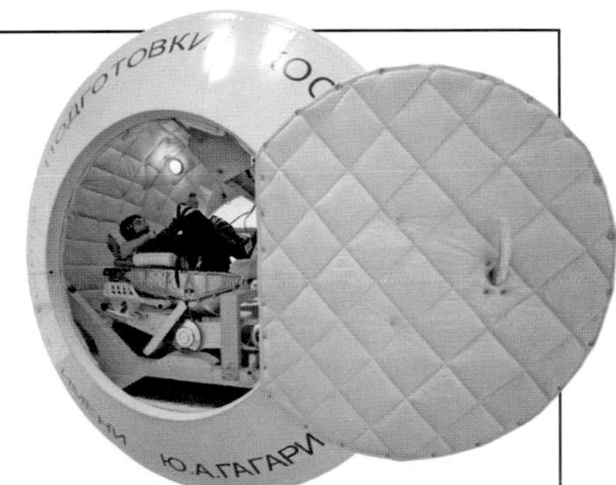

Strapped in tight
The capsule's interior has screens and controls for astronauts to practice tasks while spinning at high speeds.

POOL PRACTICE

During a mission, astronauts may need to carry out a spacewalk (see pp.118–121). Spacewalks aren't easy, so astronauts practice as much as possible on Earth beforehand. It's impossible to re-create the microgravity environment of the ISS on Earth, so training takes place in the next best thing—huge swimming pools called "neutral buoyancy" pools. The feeling of floating in water is similar to the weightlessness that astronauts experience when they're in space.

▼ Underwater replica

The Neutral Buoyancy Laboratory (NBL) in Houston, Texas, is the largest swimming pool in the US. This pool contains enough water to fill nine Olympic-sized swimming pools, but it still isn't big enough for a complete life-size replica of the ISS to fit inside.

DID YOU KNOW?

A training session in the pool can be up to seven hours long.

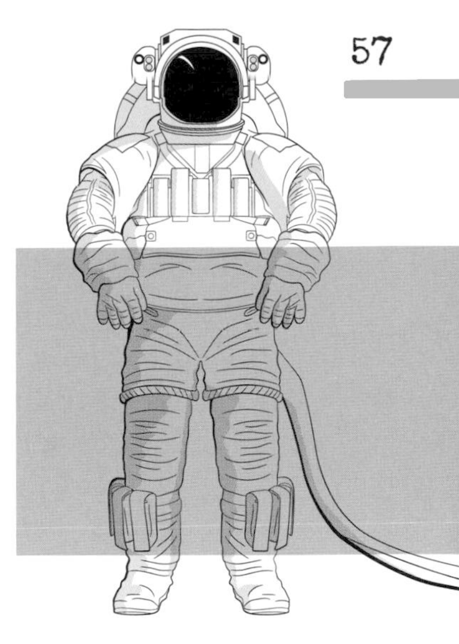

Getting dressed

On Earth, the spacesuits that astronauts wear during spacewalks seem much heavier than they do in space, and astronauts have to be helped into them, like Italian astronaut Luca Parmitano shown here. It can take as long as 45 minutes to put on a spacesuit.

Heavy lifting

Once the astronaut has put on their spacesuit, a crane is used to lift up a platform on which they stand and slowly lower them into the water. Before releasing the tethers (ropes) attaching the astronaut to the platform, support divers check that the astronaut is able to float safely in the water.

Training in water Andreas Mogensen was the first Danish astronaut to go into space. He prepared for his 2015 mission to the ISS by practising underwater at the NBL.

UNDERWATER TRAINING

A training session underwater allows astronauts to practice handling equipment they may need during a spacewalk. In the challenging environment of space, microgravity and extreme temperatures can make some tools very difficult to control. This astronaut attached a tether to a point on a replica space station before tightening the bolts; otherwise the drill's spinning motion would cause them to turn too! Practicing underwater also lets astronauts get used to their bulky spacesuit, which can be very uncomfortable after a while—the thick gloves can make even simple tasks feel tiring.

Close supervision

Several cameras provide live footage of the activities that astronauts perform underwater at the NBL. Experts monitor the screens to assess an astronaut's performance in training and also to look at any new equipment being tried out.

Safety team

A team of scuba divers supports each astronaut throughout their training session. They carry out practical tasks, such as moving astronauts around the pool, as they can't swim in their spacesuits. More importantly, the scuba divers are there to provide immediate help if an astronaut gets into difficulties in the water.

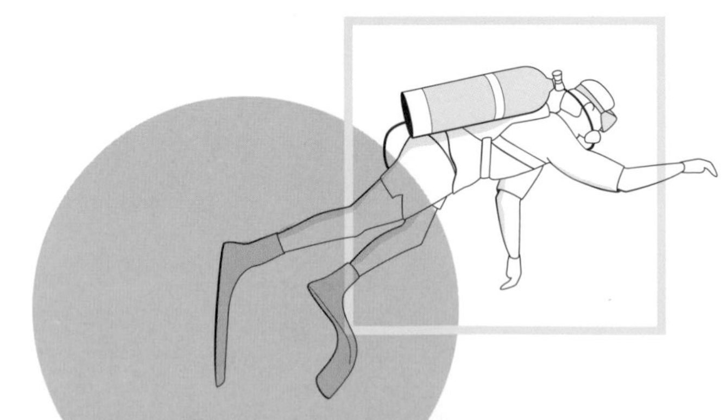

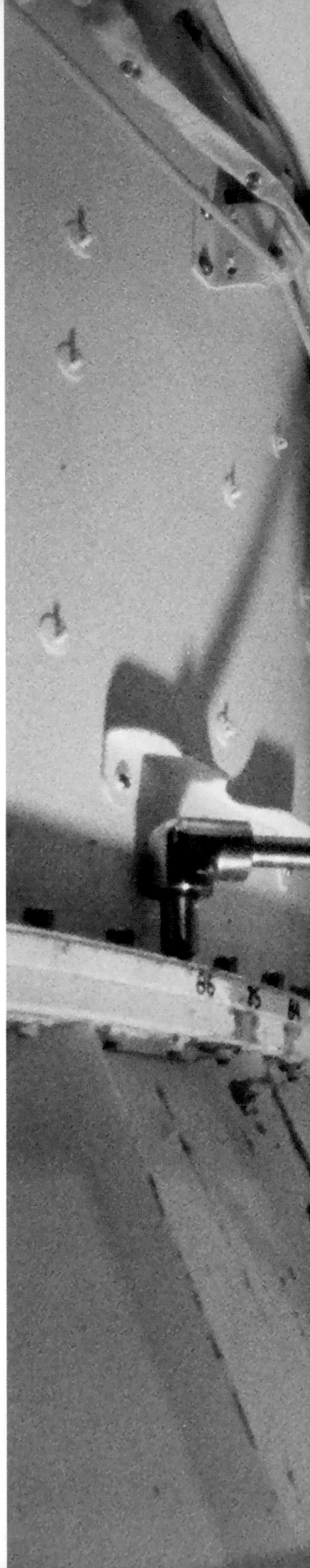

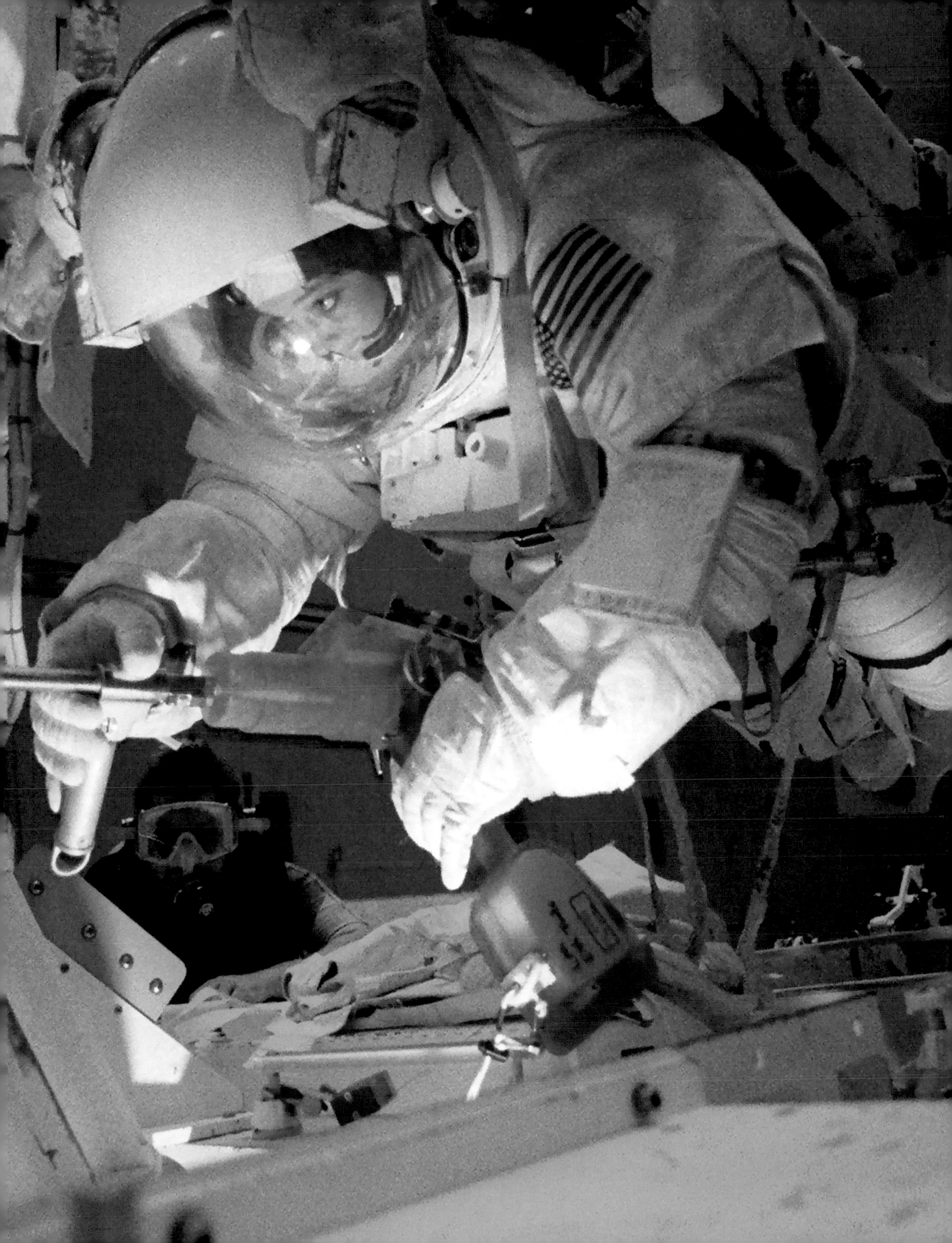

SPACE SCHOOL

Being an astronaut is one of the most exciting jobs in the world, but it requires a lot of hard work and training—they never stop learning. Anyone who is selected by NASA for training as an astronaut is called an astronaut candidate, or ASCAN for short. Before qualifying as astronauts, ASCANs spend nearly two years learning in classrooms, practicing using equipment, and undertaking outdoor challenges to improve their problem-solving skills and ability to handle difficult situations.

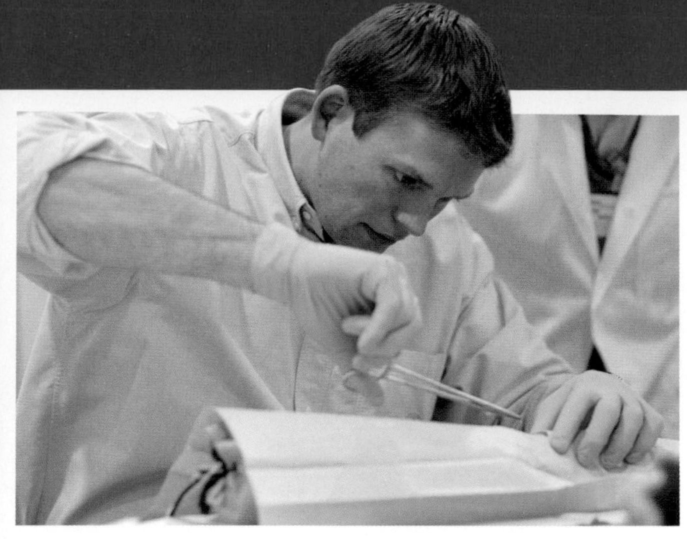

MEDICAL TRAINING

There isn't always a doctor on the space station, so astronauts must be confident in treating common medical problems, like motion sickness or aches and pains. In training, they also learn how to give injections and perform first aid, such as stitching up wounds and dealing with burn injuries.

CAVE CHALLENGE

Training in caves may seem like a strange thing to do to prepare for a mission to the ISS. However, it's actually a great way for astronauts to experience being in a confined space and practice looking out for their teammates. In 2012, astronauts discovered a new cave-dwelling crustacean, *Alpioniscus Sideralis*, during training in Sardinia, Italy.

3 weeks

The length of the ESA's cave training course for astronauts.

SURVIVAL AT SEA

The SpaceX Dragon is designed to land in the sea, and Russia's Soyuz can make emergency sea landings if something goes wrong. Astronauts must learn how to exit their spacecraft safely and keep themselves afloat and warm while waiting for help to arrive.

15 mph

The speed of the SpaceX Dragon at splashdown.

KEEPING YOUR BALANCE

Many astronauts get dizzy when first in space, as their sense of balance is disturbed. To help them adapt quickly, astronauts prepare on Earth by sitting in chairs that spin really fast and lying on tables that tilt in all directions, so that they get used to the unusual sensations they'll feel.

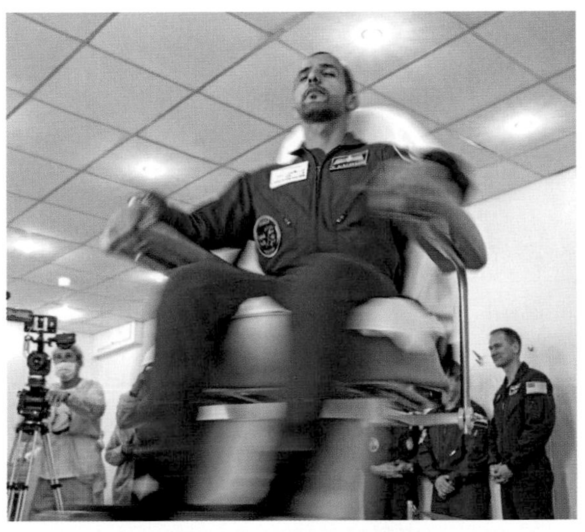

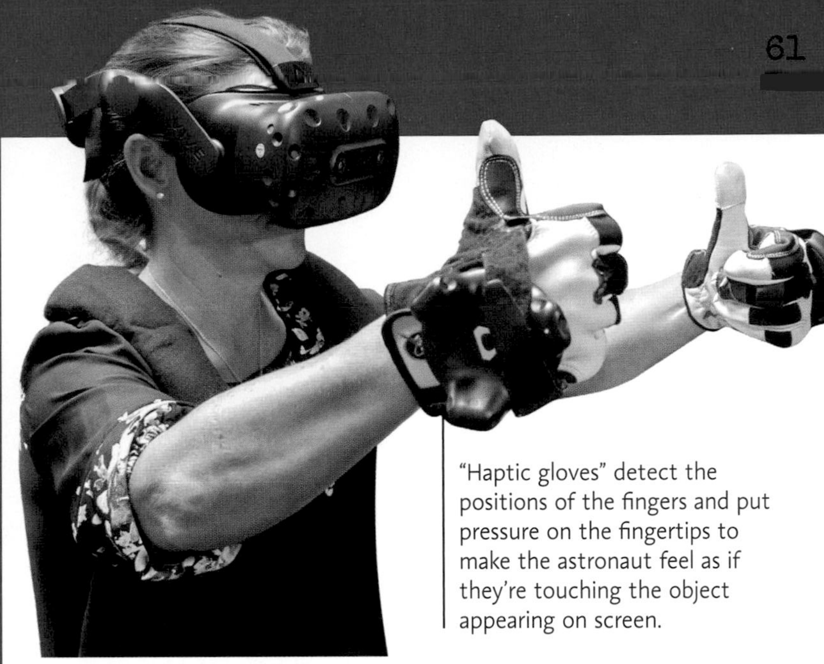

"Haptic gloves" detect the positions of the fingers and put pressure on the fingertips to make the astronaut feel as if they're touching the object appearing on screen.

VIRTUAL REALITY TRAINING

Virtual reality (VR) is an artificial world created by computers. It lets astronauts become familiar with the conditions they'll experience in space without having to leave the ground. Wearing a VR helmet and specialized gloves, astronauts do simulations in which they practice tasks, such as grabbing objects and working with tools.

CAUGHT IN THE WILD

Although scientists can roughly predict where a spacecraft will come down, astronauts must be prepared to land far away from their target, potentially even in a forest or desert. So, as part of their training, they learn how to stay safe by using only what they have in their survival packs.

BEST OF THE REST

▶ HYPOXIA TRAINING

Astronauts learn about hypoxia, a condition that occurs when the body isn't getting enough oxygen. They must be able to recognize the symptoms, such as loss of color vision, and react before they black out.

▶ SCIENTIFIC TRAINING

Not everyone who wants to be an astronaut is a scientist, so essential scientific skills, such as taking measurements, are taught in training.

▶ GEOLOGY TRAINING

Many astronauts now learn about geology—the study of rocks—in preparation for a trip to the Moon and, one day, possibly even a voyage to Mars.

Headset
All astronauts wear headsets during launch, with two microphones and two earphones, in case one breaks. Their headset allows them to speak with each other and with mission control over the noise of the spacecraft.

WHAT TO WEAR

All astronauts wear spacesuits during the most dangerous parts of a mission: launch, docking with the ISS, and landing. A spacesuit keeps the wearer safe if an emergency occurs and air is sucked out of their cabin (depressurization). Spacesuits maintain air pressure around the body and supply the wearer with oxygen for breathing.

The bright blue valve on the chest can be turned to regulate the pressure inside the suit.

The gloves are detachable.

There are two utility pockets on each leg.

▶ Sokol suit

All astronauts who fly on the Russian Soyuz wear a spacesuit known as the Sokol (meaning "falcon"). The Sokol's design hasn't changed much since it was first introduced in the 1970s.

Emergency pressure bladder
If the air pressure inside the spacecraft decreased suddenly, the pressure bladder inside the Sokol suit would automatically inflate like a balloon to protect the wearer. Without this inflated bladder, depressurization would result in unconsciousness and death.

Keeping cool

All astronauts carry a small box with them when walking to their spacecraft. This box is a portable ventilation unit, which pumps cool air into the Sokol suit. Without this unit, astronauts wouldn't be able to wear the suit for more than an hour, as their body heat can't escape—they would get too hot.

DID YOU KNOW?

Astronauts need to bend over slightly when walking in their Sokol suits because the suits are designed for sitting in, not standing.

The visor must be closed for the suit to inflate. Here, the cover is pulled down to protect the visor.

Checking for leaks

Before launch, all astronauts check their Sokol suits for any leaks by inflating them. If air were leaking out, that would reveal there was a hole. Any hole, no matter how tiny, could be disastrous if there were an emergency because the Sokol suit must be completely airtight.

Custom seats

Astronauts get shaken around during launch and reentry into Earth's atmosphere. To prevent any injuries, their seats are molded exactly to their body shapes.

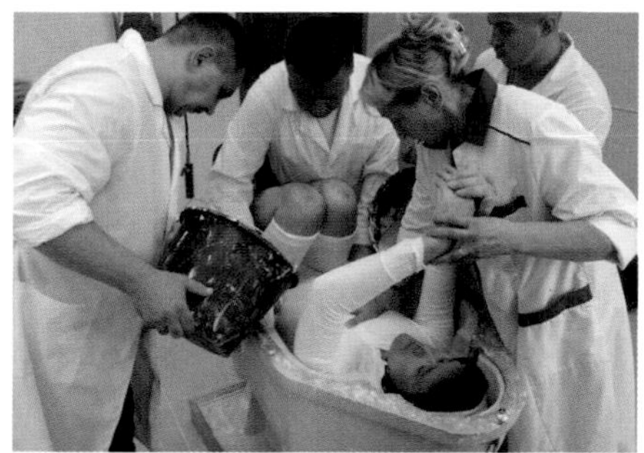

1 Measurements of the astronaut's body are taken, then they are helped into a large container. Fast-drying plaster is poured all around them.

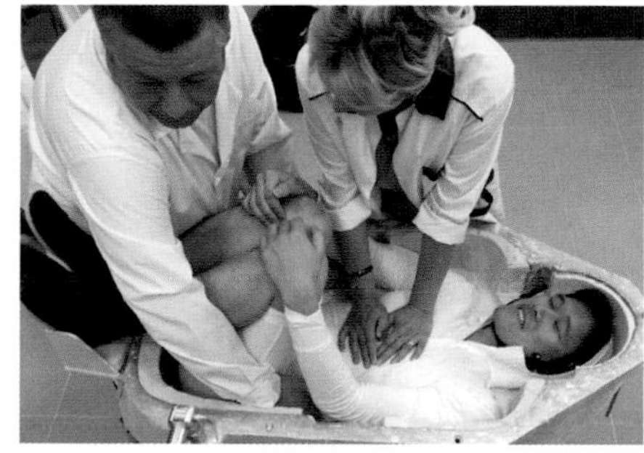

2 Seat engineers help hold the astronaut still in position while the plaster sets. The plaster mold is used to create a custom seat liner.

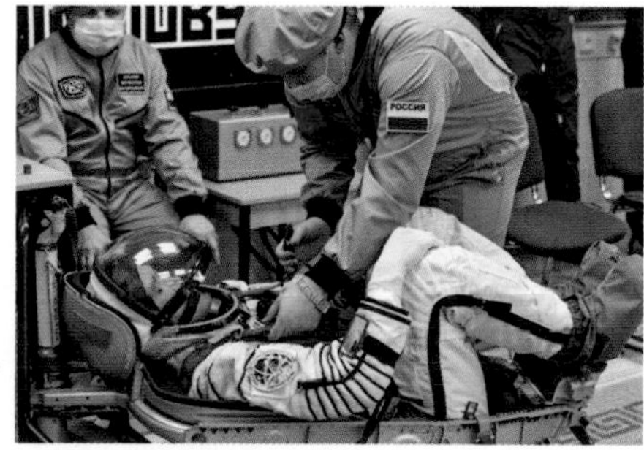

3 Once the custom seat liner has been made, the astronaut tests it out, wearing their Sokol suit, to make sure it's comfortable.

NASA
MISSION CONTROL
T/L

MISSION CONTROL

From launch through to landing, all spaceflights—crewed and uncrewed—are carefully overseen by mission controls on Earth. Mission control is home to a team of flight controllers, engineers, and support staff, led by a flight director. Around the world, mission control centers belonging to different space agencies monitor data, communicate with crews, and watch live video footage on giant screens 24 hours a day to make sure that astronauts, spacecraft, and satellites are kept safe.

◀ Johnson Space Center

The mission control center with overall responsibility for the ISS is located at NASA's Johnson Space Center (JSC) in Houston, Texas. But JSC works very closely with other space agencies in different countries to share information and plan activities for the astronauts onboard.

Other mission control centers

All space agencies have mission control centers of their own. They're in charge of all the activities and experiments carried out on their own space station modules.

RKA Mission Control Center
Known as TsUP in Russian, the RKA Mission Control Center is located at Korolev, near Moscow, Russia. It tracks the flight and landing of Soyuz spacecraft and monitors the six Russian modules of the ISS.

Tsukuba Space Center
Located near Tokyo, Japan's Tsukuba Space Center is home to its mission control. The staff there look after Japan's *Kibo* module on the ISS and all experiments carried out there.

German Space Agency (DLR)
In Europe, the German Space Agency (DLR) in Cologne, Germany, manages all activities inside the European Space Agency's *Columbus* module, the single largest module on the ISS.

LAUNCH RITUALS

Human spaceflight isn't without risk, and astronauts are a superstitious group. In the years since human spaceflight began, a number of traditions have developed—some of which are a little unusual. Following in the footsteps of earlier astronauts who carried out the same set of tasks can help those soon to leave feel part of history and more prepared for their own upcoming launch. The rituals shown here are undertaken by astronauts flying on the Russian Soyuz, but as other spacecraft capable of transporting crew are introduced, no doubt new rituals will be added to the list.

FLOWERS FOR GAGARIN

When Russian cosmonaut Yuri Gagarin, the first man is space, died, his ashes were placed in a section of the wall of the Kremlin, a huge fort in Moscow, Russia. Ever since, in the weeks before their launch, all astronauts lay red carnations under the plaque bearing his name.

BLESSING THE ROCKET

At Baikonur launchpad, Kazakhstan, a priest blesses the rocket and the astronauts. This ritual started in 1994, when Russian cosmonaut Aleksandr Viktorenko asked a priest to bless the *Soyuz TM-20* crew before they flew to the space station Mir. It has happened for every launch since.

A Russian priest sprays holy water to bless the rocket and the crew.

HOTEL DOOR SIGNING

On the day of the launch, just before leaving the Cosmonaut Hotel, all astronauts sign one of the hotel's doors. US astronaut Serena Auñón-Chancellor, shown below, carried on the tradition in 2018 before heading to her spacecraft.

PLANTING TREES

About two weeks before their mission, astronauts plant a tree in an avenue behind the Cosmonaut Hotel, Baikonur, Kazakhstan. Here, Japanese astronaut Koichi Wakata (left) and US astronaut Rick Mastracchio (right) plant a sapling.

1961

The year Russian cosmonaut Yuri Gagarin planted the first tree.

PERSONAL MASCOTS

Astronauts often carry a small, cuddly toy aboard their spacecraft for good luck and as a mascot. The toy also works as a microgravity indicator. When it starts to float around, the astronauts know that they are in microgravity too.

PRESS CONFERENCE

Astronauts and cosmonauts give a final pre-launch press conference. During this event, they talk to journalists from various news organizations. In the image above, the *Expedition 56* crew talk about the experiments that are planned for their mission and the spacewalks they will perform.

BEST OF THE REST

▶ STEAK AND EGGS

Some US astronauts choose a meal of steak and eggs, as this was what Alan Shepard, the first American in space, ate for his final meal before take-off.

▶ RUSSIAN FILM NIGHT

The night before launch, the crew gather together to watch a Russian film, *White Sun of the Desert*. This tradition dates back to *Soyuz 12* in the early 1970s.

▶ BUS-WHEEL STOP

Legend has it that the first person in space, Russian cosmonaut Yuri Gagarin, needed to pee on his bus ride to the launchpad. Since then, male astronauts have urinated on the back wheel of their transfer bus, while some female astronauts take a vial of urine with them to splash onto it.

▼ The Soyuz

The Soyuz spacecraft is 23 ft (7 m) tall and weighs nearly 7.7 tons (7 metric tons)—about the same as three rhinoceroses. Lifting it into space is the job of the almost 165 ft (50 m) tall Soyuz rocket (shown right). The Soyuz spacecraft sits at the top of the Soyuz rocket, underneath a protective nose cone known as the fairing.

1 The spacecraft and rocket are built at different sites, then transported to and assembled at Baikonur Cosmodrome, Kazakhstan. Here, the Soyuz spacecraft is being inserted into its white covering, which will be placed at the top of the Soyuz rocket.

2 The Soyuz rocket is moved from the hangar to the launchpad by rail. Local people place coins on the tracks for the train's wheels to roll over and flatten, a tradition thought to bring good luck.

3 ▶ The Soyuz rocket is raised upright by cranes, then a rehearsal takes place during which the ground crew checks that all electrical and mechanical systems are working correctly.

BAIKONUR COSMODROME, KAZAKHSTAN

The world's largest spaceport, the Baikonur Cosmodrome in Kazakhstan is used to launch all Russian spacecraft. More than 400 launches have taken place here since it was first opened in 1957.

LAUNCH DAY

After years of training and hard work, when their preparations are complete, astronauts are ready to leave Earth and launch into orbit. Introduced in 1966, the Russian Soyuz spacecraft has been carrying astronauts into space for more than 50 years. Each Soyuz (meaning "union") is only used once, so a new one is built for every journey into space. Between 2011 and 2020, it was the only vehicle in the world that could transport astronauts to the ISS.

Only three astronauts can fit in the Soyuz (see pp.136–137).

Ready to go

Astronauts arrive at the launch site more than five hours before lift-off. While engineers check the rocket, the crew get ready in their Sokol spacesuits (see pp. 62–63) and say goodbye to their families and friends.

COMMUTE TO WORK

It takes only about nine minutes from lift-off for the astronauts to reach space. As the rocket starts moving upward, the astronauts inside feel it shake powerfully. Then, anywhere between three hours and two days later, they dock with the ISS.

3... 2... 1... Lift-off!

Two-and-a-half hours before lift-off, the astronauts take their seats, and 35 minutes later, the hatch is closed. Twenty-nine seconds before lift-off, the rocket's main engines are fired—the exhaust gases are pushed downward, propelling the rocket upward.

Blasted into space
A fully loaded Soyuz rocket, like this one that launched from Baikonur launchpad, Kazakhstan, in 2008, is about as heavy as 60 elephants when it takes off.

4 Orbital spaceflight
About nine minutes after lift-off, the spacecraft enters Earth's orbit. Its solar panels open up as soon as it's in space.

3 Third stage
Five minutes after lift-off, when the fuel in the second stage has run out, the engines in the third section start working.

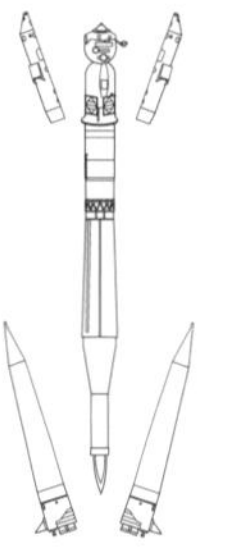

2 Second stage
Two minutes after lift-off, the upper protective cover of the rocket and the boosters, which provide extra power for lift-off, fall away. The engines in the second stage are fired up.

1 First stage
The first stage is fired up just before lift-off and has enough fuel to burn for two minutes.

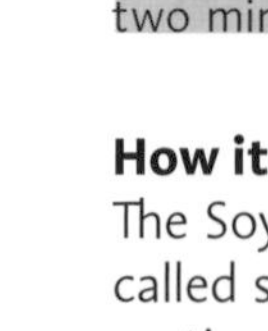

How it works
The Soyuz rocket is made up of three sections, called stages, each with its own engines. As each section runs out of fuel, it detaches from the rocket, making it lighter as it travels upward.

▲ Meeting in the middle

Like the ISS, the Soyuz is moving incredibly fast, so the astronauts have to be very careful when docking. The pilot gradually matches the speed of the Soyuz to that of the ISS and then slowly moves closer until the Soyuz is close enough to attach itself.

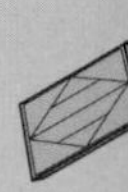

Parked up
After the Soyuz docks with the space station, it is left parked there until the crew is ready to return to Earth.

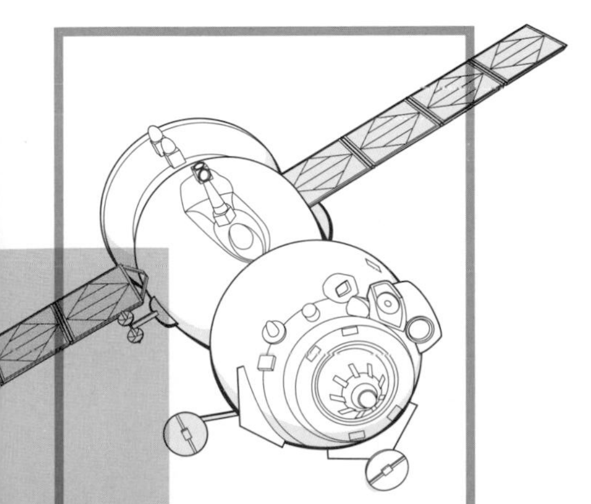

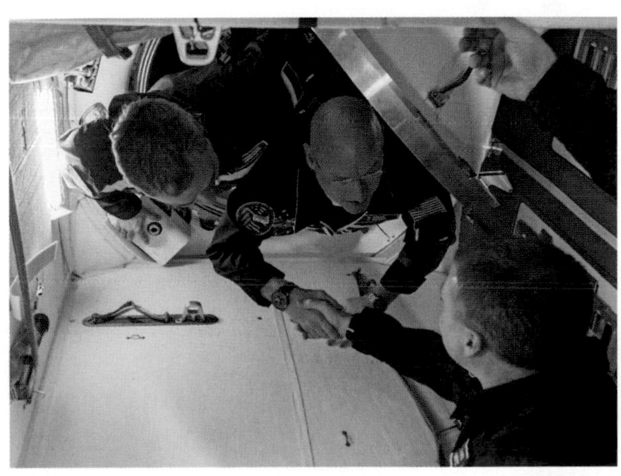

Space greeting

A knock at the door is very exciting, as it's rare to receive visitors on the space station. In this image, US astronaut Scott Kelly (top right) and Russian cosmonaut Mikhail Kornienko (top left) float out of the Soyuz to be welcomed by US astronaut Terry Virts aboard the ISS on March 28, 2015.

CREW DRAGON

Founded by the South African–born multibillionaire Elon Musk, SpaceX is a company that designs, builds, and launches rockets and spacecraft. It became the first privately owned company to send a cargo spacecraft to the space station in 2012, and in 2020, its partly reusable Dragon 2 spacecraft began taking crews to the ISS. It can also carry up to 6.6 tons (6 metric tons) of cargo.

Ready for launch

The 230 ft (70 m) two-stage rocket used to launch the Dragon capsule is known as the Falcon 9 Block 5. SpaceX's Falcon 9 rockets are named after the "Millennium Falcon," the fictional starship in the *Star Wars* films.

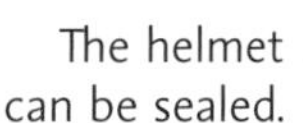

The helmet can be sealed.

The suit is fire-resistant.

SpaceX suit

The crew wear spacesuits in flight to protect them in case of emergencies. Since they won't be fully exposed to space, the suit design can be relatively lightweight and flexible.

▼ All aboard

In April 2021, four astronauts boarded the Dragon capsule *Endeavour* for SpaceX's Crew-2 mission to the ISS. In contrast to the cluttered interiors of earlier spacecraft, Dragon is relatively spacious. There's even room for a closed-off toilet area.

LC-39A

SpaceX launches its crewed missions from Launch Complex 39A (LC-39A) at the Kennedy Space Center in Florida —the launchpad for the Apollo lunar missions and the space shuttle. Rockets are assembled at a horizontal integration facility (HIF) nearby.

At the controls
While Dragon mostly flies under automatic control, each flight still carries a fully trained pilot.

From launch to docking

Dragon launches inside a protective nose cone on top of the Falcon 9 rocket. It takes about a day for the capsule to reach the station.

1 The Falcon 9's lower rocket stage fires to launch Dragon. After two minutes, the engine cuts out, and it separates and falls away from the upper stage.

2 The lower stage makes a controlled return to Earth, using its remaining fuel to make an upright landing so that it can be repaired and reused.

3 Boosted into space by the upper stage, Dragon aims for the ISS. It matches speed with the station and docks automatically.

SPACE TRANSPORT

From the earliest days of the ISS, space agencies needed reliable vehicles to transport crews and cargo safely back and forth between Earth and space. Russia's most reliable spacecraft haven't changed much for decades, but the retirement of the space shuttle in 2011 forced the US to design new vehicles to replace it. Meanwhile, China has continued to develop its space transport at a faster rate than any other nation. The older spacecraft shown here were designed to be expendable (used only once), but more recent US vehicles, such as Dragon and Orion, have reusable crew modules.

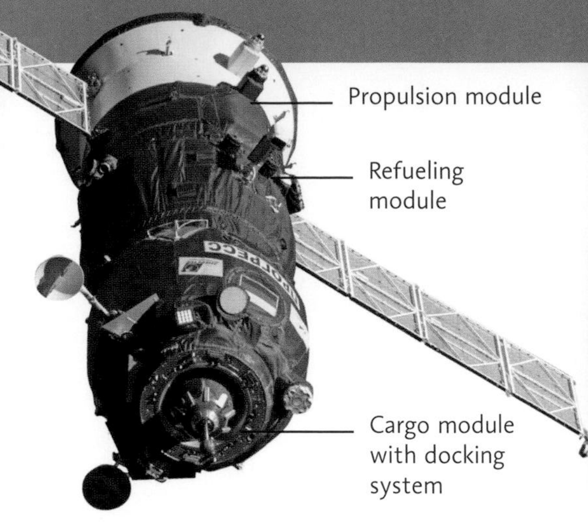

PROGRESS

Regarded as the space station workhorses, Russia's Progress spacecraft are unpiloted versions of Soyuz spacecraft. Since 2000, they have averaged three to four trips to the ISS per year.

1978

The year the Progress spacecraft made its first flight.

BOEING STARLINER

Made up of a reusable crew capsule and an expendable service module, the US's Starliner will carry up to seven astronauts to low Earth orbit or up to four to the ISS.

Test landing
Huge airbags inflate to soften the landing of a test capsule.

TIANZHOU

First launched in 2017, Tianzhou ("heavenly ship") is an unpiloted spacecraft supplying China's space station, Tiangong. As an expendable ship, it burns up in the atmosphere on return.

14,300

The weight of cargo in pounds that the Tianzhou spacecraft can transport.

CYGNUS

Designed for cargo missions to the ISS, the unpiloted Cygnus first flew in 2013 and is the US equivalent of the Progress spacecraft. After resupplying the ISS, Cygnus is loaded with garbage to burn up with the spacecraft as it reenters Earth's atmosphere.

SOYUZ

In use since the 1960s, the Russian-built Soyuz is an expendable spacecraft. Between 2011 and 2020, it was the only spacecraft able to transport astronauts to the ISS. Additionally, since 2000, a Soyuz has always been docked on the ISS for use as a "lifeboat" in the event of an emergency.

SPACEX DRAGON

In use from 2010 to 2020, SpaceX's partly reusable Cargo Dragon was the first privately built spacecraft to return safely from orbit. It could transport 7,300 lb (3,300 kg) of goods. In 2020, it was replaced by the Dragon 2, which has two types—one carries cargo and the other crew.

Docked at ISS
Canadarm2 grabs the Dragon capsule and helps it dock to the ISS.

BEST OF THE REST

▶ KOUNOTORI

First launched in 2009, this unpiloted expendable Japanese cargo spacecraft made nine supply missions to the ISS before its retirement in 2020.

▶ SHENZHOU

Based on the design of the Russian Soyuz, the Chinese spacecraft Shenzhou has carried cargo to space since 1999 and crew since 2003.

▶ ORION

Orion is the vehicle for NASA's future Space Launch System (SLS), its most powerful rocket yet. When it launches, it will take up to four astronauts farther into space than anyone has ever traveled before.

ROLES BEHIND THE SCENES

FLIGHT DIRECTOR

On Earth, the person in charge of managing the space station and the teams supporting it is known as the flight director. It's a varied role that includes monitoring the mission and having the final say in decisions that need to be made. When there is a problem, it's the job of the flight director to make quick and informed decisions, with support from the team, to protect the astronauts and the space station too.

Screen time

The flight director receives regular reports from the flight controllers, who monitor data coming in from the space station. The flight controllers work in shifts covering days, nights, and weekends to spot any problems or answer questions.

Other roles in mission control

Operating the ISS is a complex job, and the flight director can't manage it all alone. A large team of people with different skills and expertise help keep the station safe. For example, flight surgeons look after the physical and mental health of the crew, navigation experts track the station, and robotics officers watch over the station's robotic arm.

CAPCOM
The Capsule Communicator (CAPCOM) is one of the very few people to speak directly with the astronauts. This role is usually taken by another astronaut.

Flight controller
About a dozen flight controllers work at mission control at a time. Each one has a specific role, like looking after docking or coordinating spacewalks.

Public affairs officer
This person is the public face of the ISS. They share exciting stories about launches and activities on the ISS and keep the public up-to-date with space news.

It takes a while to get used to living on the space station. When astronauts first arrive, they can be a little clumsy; learning how to move well in microgravity takes practice. Once settled in, astronauts follow a strict daily schedule, filled with tasks set by mission control—from keeping the station clean and tidy to exercising for two hours to keep their muscles, hearts, and bones strong. Life on board the space station is busy, but there are quiet moments for admiring the spectacular view too. In the evening, dinner times are an opportunity for the crew to relax together and enjoy the unique experience of trying to eat their food before it floats away!

4 LIFE ON BOARD

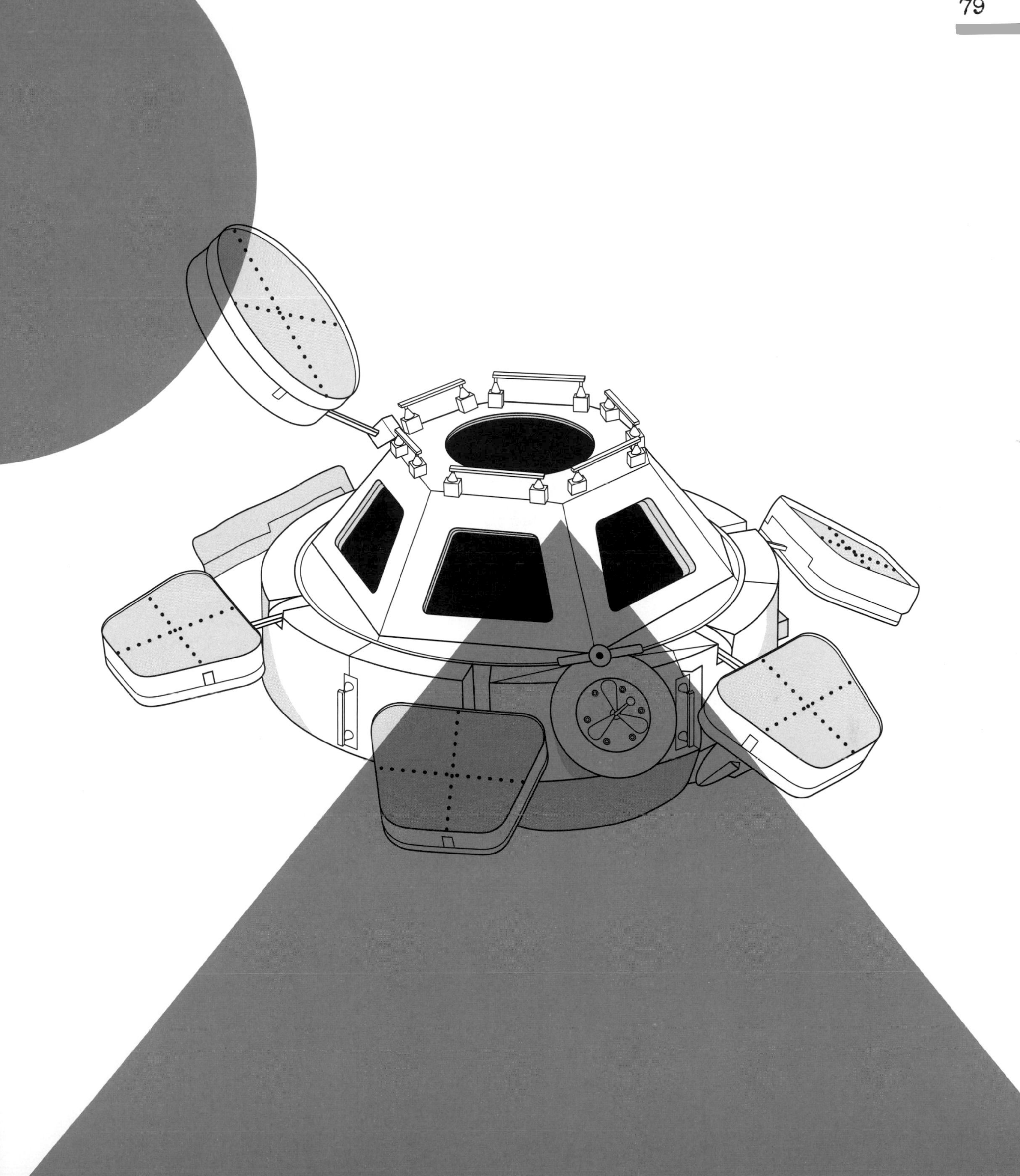

DID YOU KNOW?

All the writing on the walls of the ISS faces in the same direction so that everyone can agree which way is up.

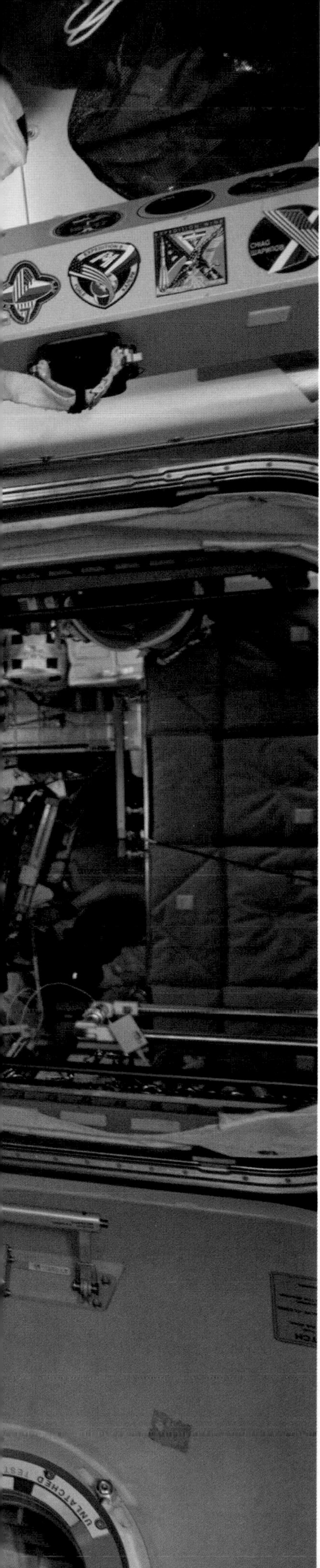

WHICH WAY IS UP?

After traveling to space in a cramped capsule, it's only when they board the ISS that astronauts experience the full effect of microgravity. Anything that isn't buckled down floats around—even the astronauts themselves. It's a confusing experience, and at first they often feel dizzy or sick. After a few days, however, they overcome this "space adaptation syndrome" and learn the advantages—and disadvantages—of life in orbit.

◀ Up or down?

The space station has a lot to fit in, but since there's no difference between a floor, a wall, or a ceiling, every surface can be crammed with equipment. Surfaces are labeled so that astronauts can find their way around and locate what they need.

Small tasks, big effort

Astronauts can often find themselves struggling to do simple tasks without things floating away. For this reason, there are footholds, straps, and plenty of Velcro to help astronauts keep themselves and their equipment in place.

In space, pockets and Velcro are essential for keeping objects from floating away; astronauts often wear shorts or trousers with Velcro pieces on them.

Looping their feet under foot rails helps astronauts stay anchored.

TASTE TEST

Astronauts often say that their sense of taste changes in space and that it can be tricky to eat in microgravity. In the past, missions to space lasted just a few days, so food didn't matter that much. Nowadays, with missions lasting months, tasty meals are essential for keeping astronauts feeling happy, healthy, and able to work. Before a mission, astronauts work with food scientists to decide which dishes they'd like to take with them.

Scorecard
Astronauts score possible dishes based on several factors, such as flavor, texture, appearance, and smell.

DID YOU KNOW?

Russian cosmonaut Yuri Gagarin ate the first food in space: caviar and pâté.

Celebratory meal preparations

Since 2006, famous French chef Alain Ducasse has been providing European astronauts with fancy meals suitable for celebrations in orbit. Like typical space meals, these special ones must also last a long time and be safe for astronauts to eat in space.

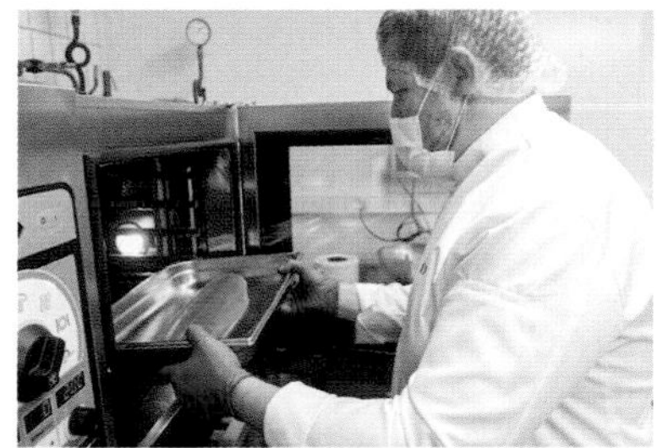

1 Ducasse's team members maintain cleanliness by wearing masks, gloves, and head caps while handling the food.

2 Pieces of the cooked food are placed into cans and sauces are added before the can lids are sealed in place.

3 Sealed cans are exposed to radiation to kill dangerous bacteria to reduce the risk of tummy bugs in space.

4 After packaging and cleaning, the sealed cans are ready to be transported to the launch facility.

▲ Try before you fly

Many astronauts soon to visit the ISS go to NASA's Space Food Systems Laboratory in Houston, Texas, to try various dishes and select their favorite foods for the mission. Some foods are banned from the ISS, such as bread and potato chips, as they create crumbs.

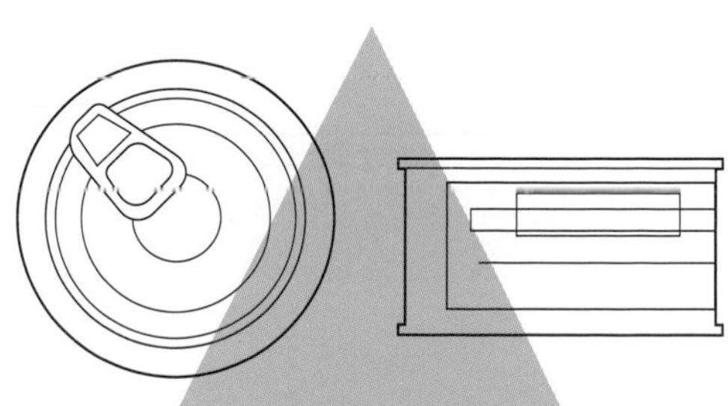

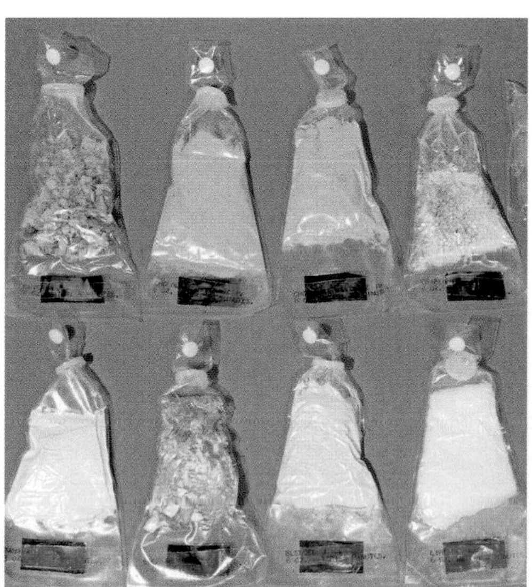

Tubed, cubed, or powdered?

In the 1960s, astronauts on NASA's Project Mercury had dishes like mushroom soup, chicken with gravy, and beef with vegetables, as well as pears and strawberries. These were served in unappetizing-looking tubes as paste, turned into bite-sized cubes, or powdered.

▶ Setting the table

The ISS has two kitchen areas, known as galleys—one in the Russian *Zvezda* module and one in the US *Unity* module. The *Unity* galley has a specially adapted dining table. It's hard to eat when everything keeps floating out of reach, so the table has strips of Velcro that are used to secure packets, bottles, and utensils in place.

Nuts, granola bars, and cookies are no-fuss foods.

Antibacterial wipes help with cleaning up any spills.

Foods like soup and eggs are packed in vacuum-sealed pouches with all the air and water removed, so they last longer.

WHAT'S FOR DINNER?

Mealtimes in space are rather different than dinners at home on Earth. In microgravity, food floats away if it's not secured in place, and you can't drink from a cup—the liquid inside wouldn't pour like it does on Earth. During long missions, food plays an important role in keeping astronauts happy and healthy. Scientists and engineers have come up with some clever ways to make eating and drinking in space as enjoyable as possible.

BIG MOMENT

Pizza party
In 2001, restaurant chain Pizza Hut arranged for an out-of-this-world pizza delivery to the ISS. Russian cosmonaut Yuri Usachev was recorded happily munching on a slice.

Spicy condiments are kept in little bottles.

Scissors are used to cut open packets of food.

Drinking in space

Astronauts drink from pouches with straws instead of cups. The drink pouches have a screw cap, much like the one on a toothpaste tube, which can be closed to prevent any liquid from escaping.

Prepping the food

Some space meals, such as macaroni and cheese, come in dehydrated (dried) form. Astronauts attach their food or drink pouch to the galley's rehydration station and fill it with hot or cold water. Many food items, like ham or chicken, can be thermostabilized—they're heated to destroy any harmful microbes, then sealed in airtight packages. Astronauts reheat these foods in a specially designed oven before eating.

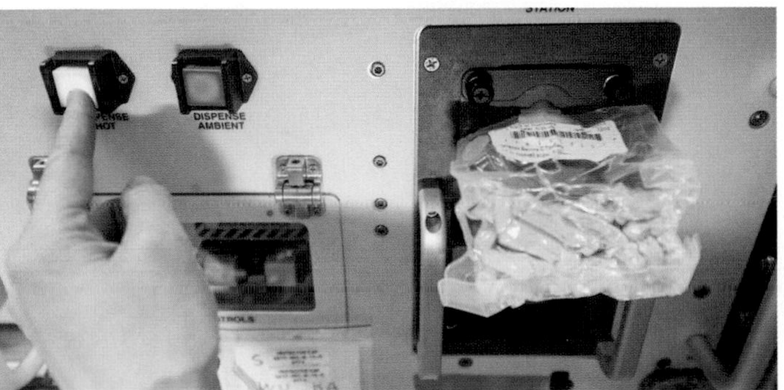

Astronaut favorites

In microgravity, bodily fluids collect in astronauts' upper bodies, including in their heads. This reduces their sense of taste, so their favorite meals often have strong, spicy flavors.

Shrimp cocktail
The zingy sauce on this seafood dish has made it an astronaut favorite ever since the first humans went to space.

Space tacos
Bread can't be eaten in space, as the crumbs can get stuck in the space station's systems. Tacos made out of tortillas make a great alternative, and sauces can help hold down other ingredients.

Ramen noodles
The microgravity version of this spicy noodle soup has been a favorite on the ISS ever since Japanese astronaut Soichi Noguchi brought it with him to the station in 2005.

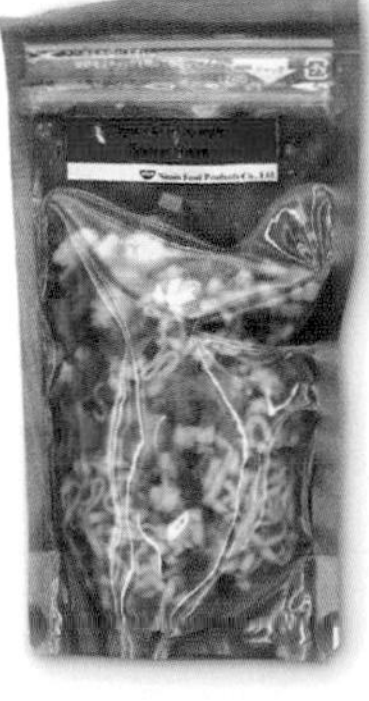

FOOD SWAPS

On October 1, 2019, the crew of Expedition 60 gathered for a celebratory meal in the *Zvezda* module to welcome new crewmates, US astronaut Jessica Meir, Russian cosmonaut Oleg Skripochka, and Emirati astronaut Hazza Al Mansouri. For astronauts, eating together is a great opportunity to bond as a team and to relax after a hard day's work. It's also a chance to share dishes from their own country and try food from others. Astronauts from all over the world visit the space station, and while NASA and Russian space agency Roscosmos supply most of the food, other space agencies often send up their own national delicacies.

Expanding the menu

When astronaut Koichi Wakata became the space station's first Japanese resident in 2009, he arrived with 28 new dishes developed by Japanese space agency JAXA. These dishes helped expand the menu on the ISS to about 200 choices.

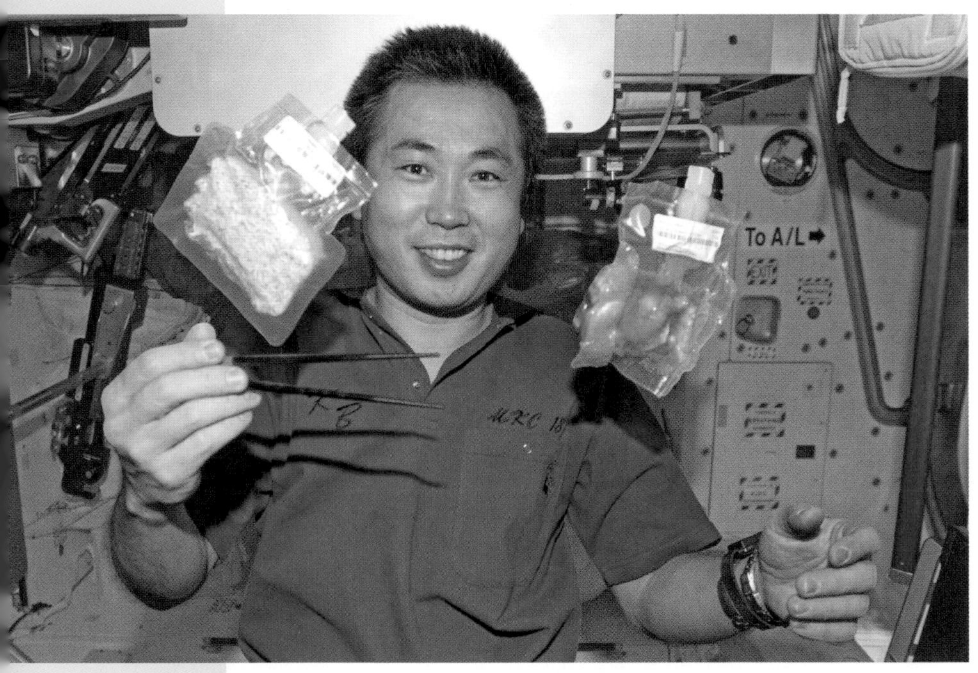

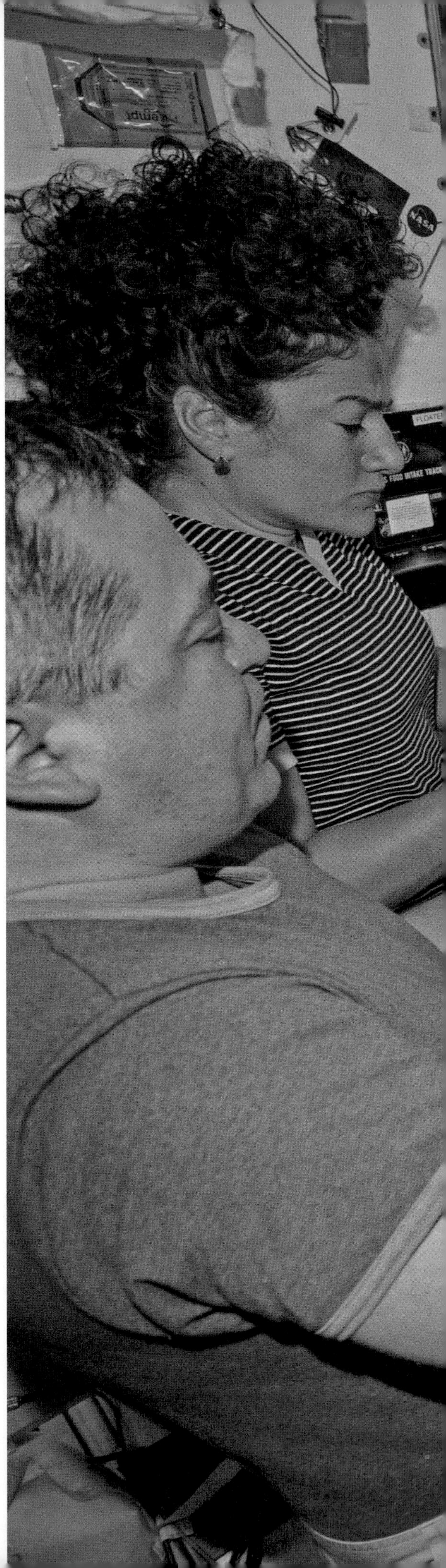

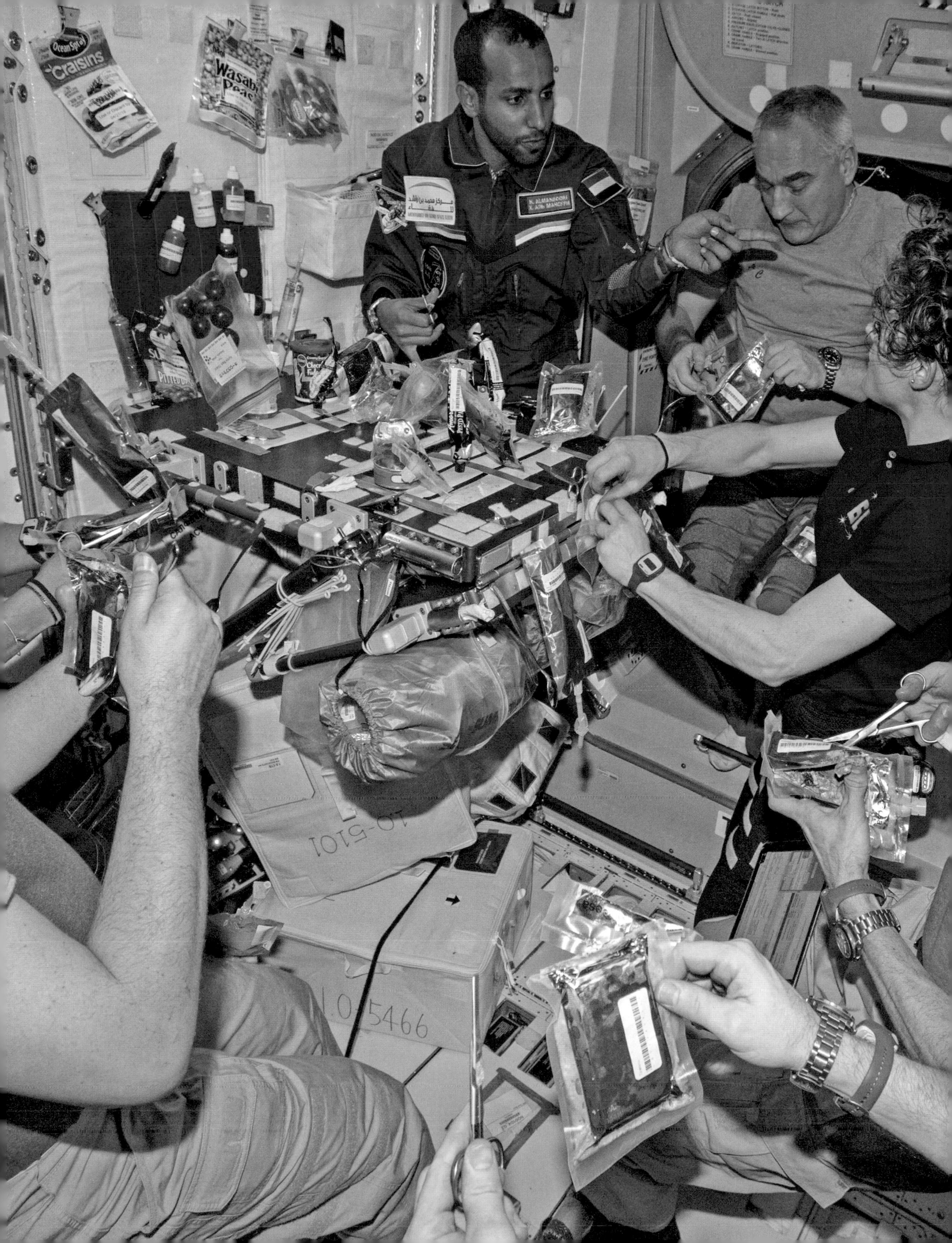
Ocean Spray
Craisins
Wasabi Peas

FRESH SUPPLIES

From crew members and equipment to food and water, everything needed for life in space must be sent from Earth. To keep the station supplied, automated spacecraft are launched regularly by various space agencies. Some of these spacecraft return to Earth to be reused, while others burn up in Earth's atmosphere after making their deliveries.

DID YOU KNOW?

A Kounotori can carry cargo equal in weight to a large elephant.

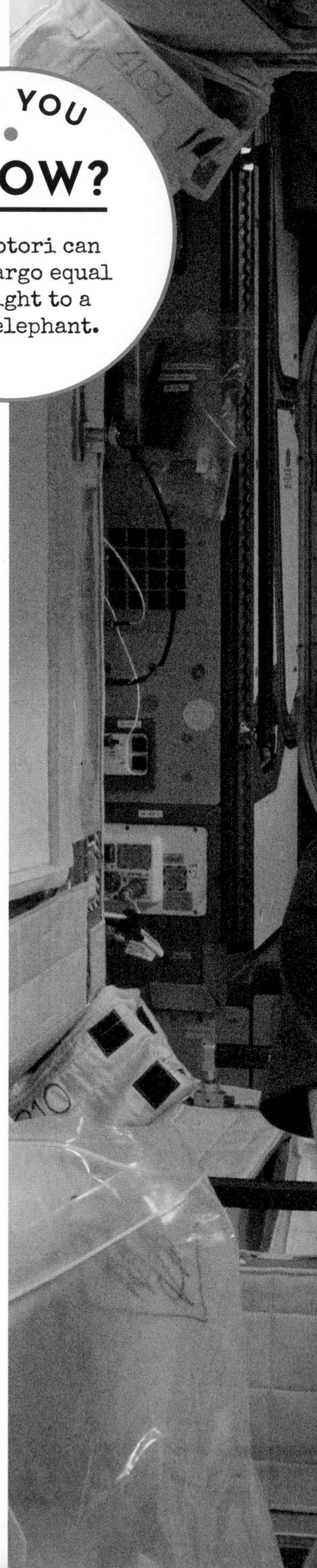

Transporting cargo

A variety of uncrewed spacecraft supply the ISS, including Japan's Kounotori—meaning "white stork." These automated spacecraft are just under 33 ft (10 m) long.

1 Items for use onboard the station are packed in lightweight containers that are stacked on pallets before they are carefully loaded into Kounotori.

Kounotori has an exterior cargo bay too, which can be emptied by Canadarm2.

2 An H-IIB rocket with Kounotori sitting at the top is launched from Tanageshima Launch Complex in southern Japan.

3 Astronauts on the station monitor Kounotori as it gradually approaches and settles into an orbit close to that of the ISS.

4 The station crew use the Canadarm2 robotic arm to grab Kounotori and guide it in to connect with a docking port on the *Harmony* module.

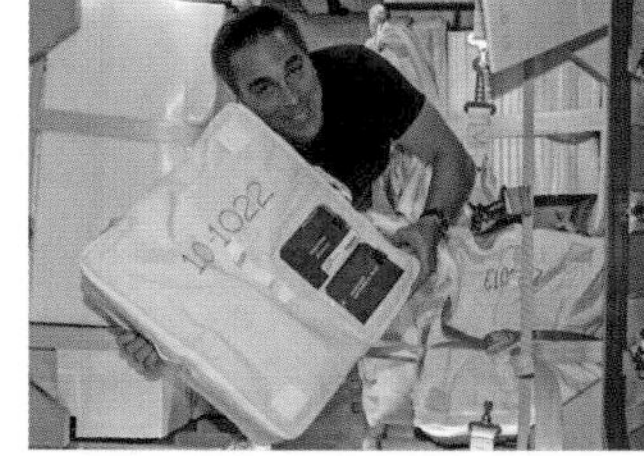

5 Kounotori is unloaded, then filled up again with station waste, and sent back toward Earth. The spacecraft burns up as it reenters the atmosphere.

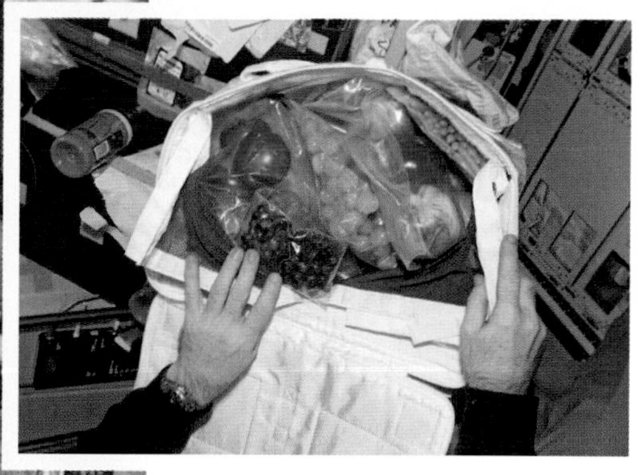

◀ Juicy treats

Fresh fruit and vegetables in a cargo delivery are a welcome sight to astronauts far from home. With limited space for keeping food cool, fruit and vegetables have a short shelf life, but they give astronauts some variety at mealtimes while they last. There's also room onboard for sweets and other treats—and sometimes even carefully packaged ice cream.

BIG MOMENT

Station supplies briefly seemed in danger after both a Progress module and a SpaceX Cargo Dragon (below) malfunctioned en route to the ISS in April and June 2015. However, the crisis was averted by successful Kounotori and Progress missions later that year.

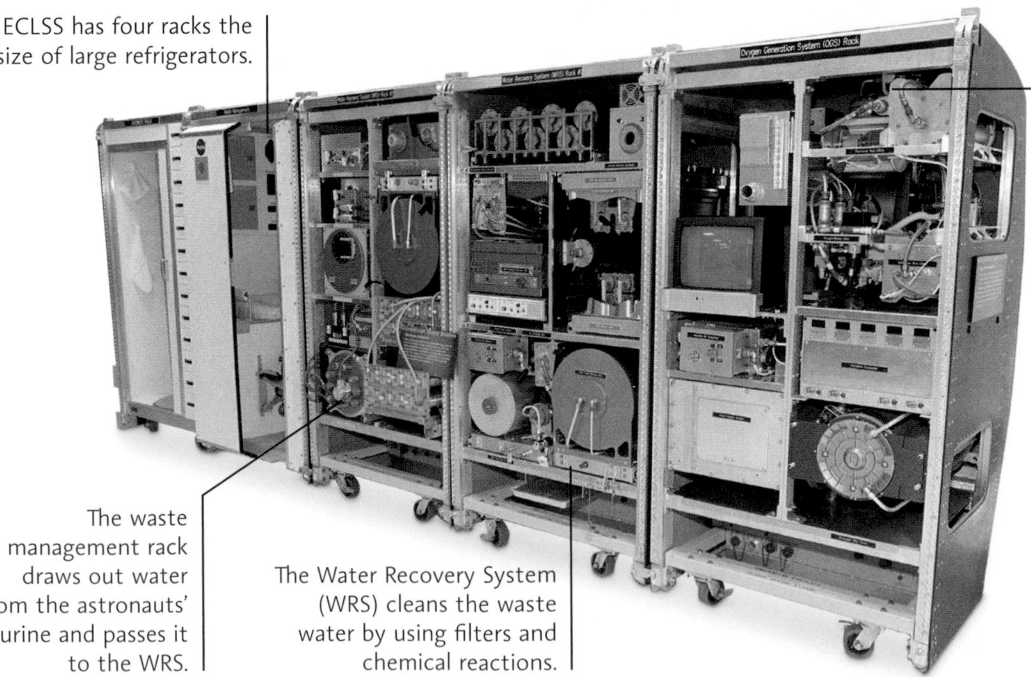

ECLSS has four racks the size of large refrigerators.

The Oxygen Generation System (OGS) uses electricity to break down water into oxygen that astronauts can breathe and hydrogen.

The waste management rack draws out water from the astronauts' urine and passes it to the WRS.

The Water Recovery System (WRS) cleans the waste water by using filters and chemical reactions.

Life support

Systems such as the Environmental Control and Life Support System (ECLSS) racks on the *Tranquility* module provide the crew with clean air and water and recycle their waste.

CHORES IN SPACE

It's easy for the space station to start feeling a little untidy or even dirty: objects in microgravity don't stay where they're supposed to, and microbes (tiny living organisms) brought from Earth by visiting astronauts can get everywhere in weightless conditions. To ensure the station remains a pleasant place to live, astronauts schedule a few hours each week to give their home a good cleaning.

Out of control
This dish with fungi samples from the ISS shows what happens when microbes grow unchecked. Some of these microbes could potentially pose a health risk to astronauts on board. The specific microbes living in a particular place are referred to collectively as a microbiome; the ISS microbiome includes 55 different types of microbes.

◀ Cleaning day

Microbes can be found anywhere on board—in stray bubbles of drinks, food crumbs, and droplets from coughs and sneezes. Here, US astronaut Jack Fisher cleans the cupola carefully with antimicrobial wipes to prevent microbes from collecting on its parts.

Housekeeping tasks

Every Saturday, the crew give the space station a thorough cleaning. All the main modules are vacuumed, and all surfaces are cleaned with disinfectant wipes. Astronauts take turns cleaning the messiest modules, like the dining and exercise areas.

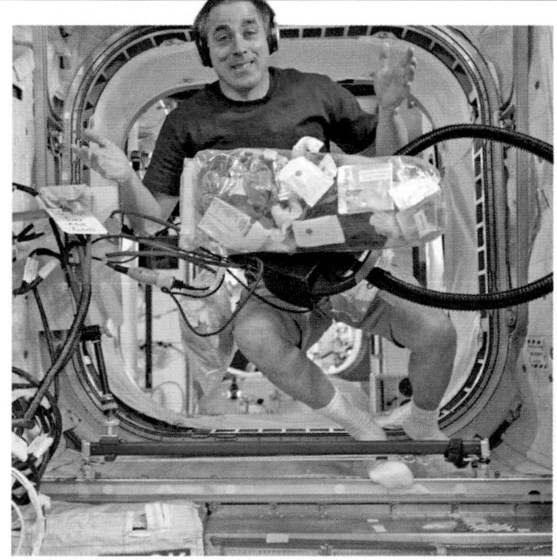

Taking out the trash
Most garbage is packed into bags and loaded into a cargo spacecraft that will burn up in Earth's atmosphere.

Vacuuming
The station's vacuum cleaner is used to clean the air filters, where dust and dirt tend to collect.

DID YOU

KNOW?

Some astronauts use supplements of melatonin, a hormone that helps promote sleep, to keep the rhythm of day and night.

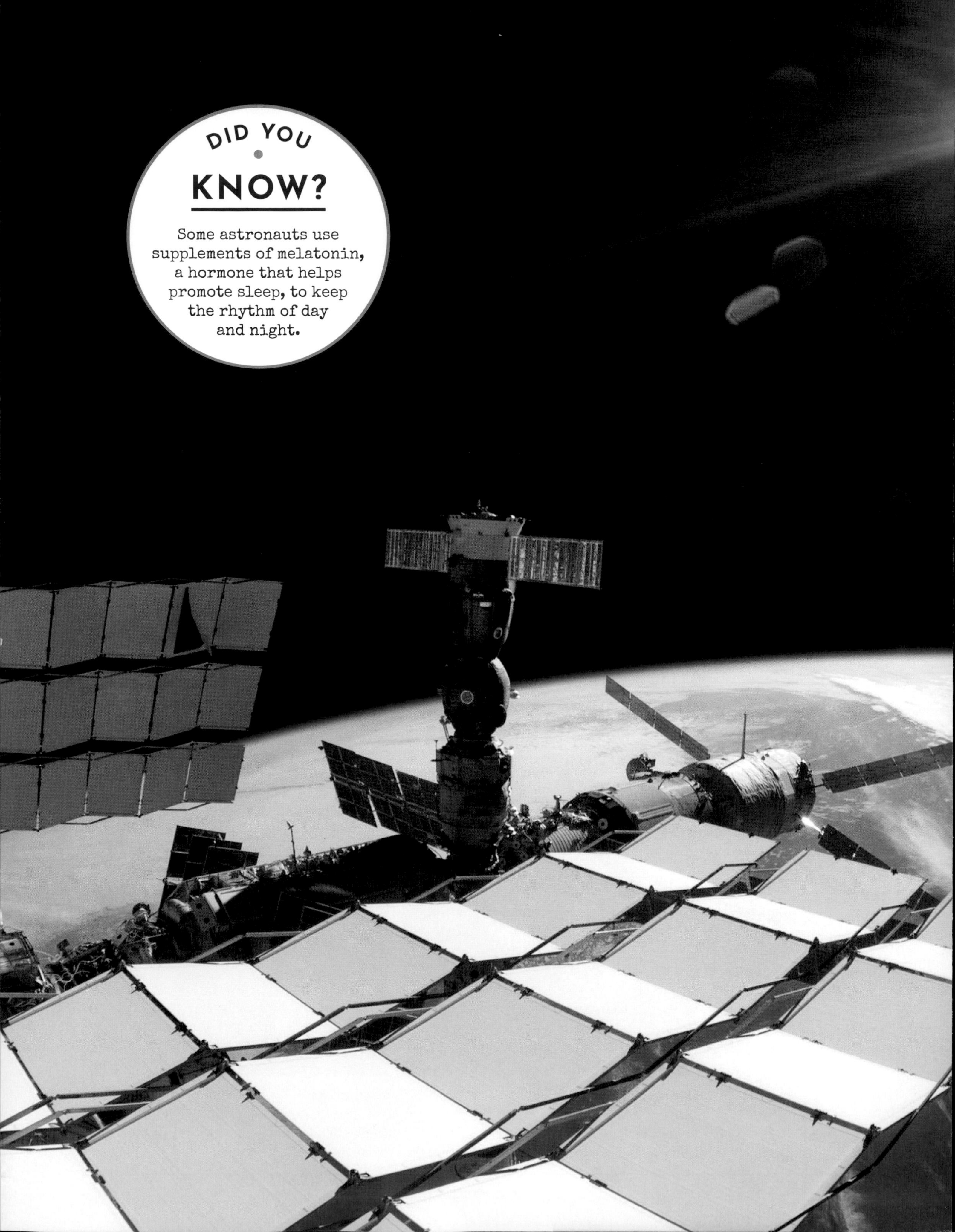

SUNRISE

Orbiting Earth once every 93 minutes, the space station experiences 16 sunrises and 16 sunsets for every Earth day. It's a spectacular sight, but so many sunrises in a day can easily upset the astronauts' sleep patterns. Fortunately, the amount of sunlight entering the station through windows is limited, so artificial lighting is used to structure the crew's day.

Morning view
US astronaut Terry Virts watches a sunrise from the cupola. Coatings on the windows filter out dangerous ultraviolet rays, but the Sun's glare can still be intense, and crew members often wear sunglasses.

Time flies

Disrupting a person's daily rhythms can affect their ability to judge periods of time accurately. An altered sense of time can be a problem on the space station, where astronauts follow a strict schedule that divides their days into five-minute segments. Using a virtual reality (VR) headset, US astronaut Victor Glover is testing how life in orbit affects his time perception and reaction speeds.

◀ Extreme temperatures

The space station experiences huge temperature differences with each day–night cycle since it's exposed to intense heat and then plunged into chilly darkness. Layers of reflective insulation help shield it from the Sun's searing rays, while ammonia-filled radiators (the white rectangles shown here) are used to send the station's excess heat out into space.

THE CUPOLA

The space station cupola was a spectacular new addition to the ISS when it arrived in 2010. Mounted on the Earth-facing side (nadir) of the *Tranquility* module, its hexagonal bubble shape and large windows provide astronauts with great views of Earth as well as the station exterior and visiting spacecraft.

The shutters can easily be opened and closed by astronauts inside the cupola.

▶ Admiring the view

The cupola has six side windows and an overhead one that is 31.5 in (80 cm) across. Crew members use it to photograph Earth, conduct experiments, and monitor incoming spacecraft during docking. There is also a control station for the robotic arm Canadarm2, which can be viewed through the windows.

DID YOU KNOW?

The term cupola comes from the Italian word for "dome"—and is more often used to describe a domelike structure on top of a cathedral.

Inside the cupola

The module has become a favorite place for astronauts to relax and reconnect with Earth. However, banks of monitors, controls, and cables beneath the windows reveal that it's also an important working part of the station.

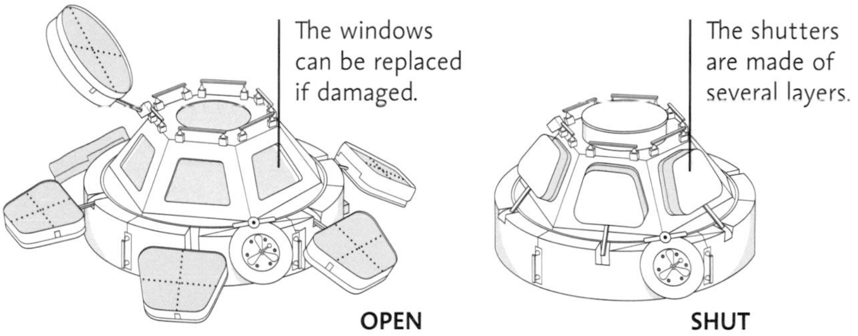

Each window consists of four layers of toughened "bulletproof" glass to limit the damage caused by any micrometeorites or flying space debris.

The windows can be replaced if damaged.

The shutters are made of several layers.

OPEN

SHUT

Open or shut?

The cupola's shutters are kept closed when it's not in use, to protect the windows from space debris. Closed shutters also protect against cosmic radiation from the Sun and keep the station's temperature constant by preventing it from heating up in direct sunlight or losing heat into the vacuum of space during darkness.

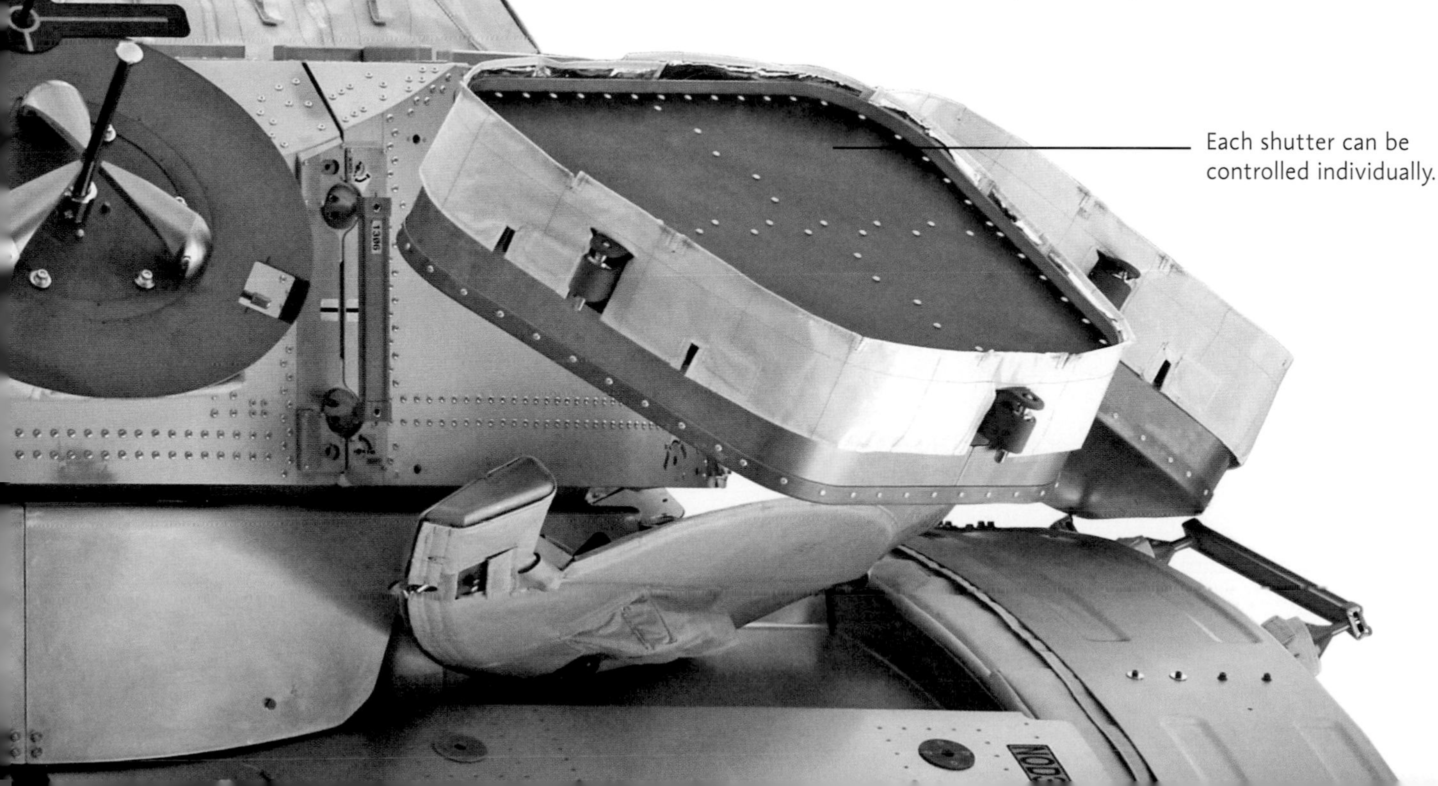

Each shutter can be controlled individually.

Photographic moments

Astronauts learn how to handle cameras as part of their training, and many find that photography becomes a favorite hobby during their time on the space station. With their unique perspective, astronauts provide scientists with useful images of fast-changing phenomena, such as hurricanes or erupting volcanoes.

▶ Earth from space

The space station's altitude gives a much closer view of Earth than satellites in higher orbits. Using handheld cameras and automated equipment, its crew can take photos revealing Earth's beauty. This view of Egypt, for instance, shows the dark strip of the Nile Valley (left of center) surrounded by desert and the clouds over the Mediterranean Sea.

SPACE SNAPS

From around 250 miles (400 km) above Earth, the space station provides an amazing vantage point. The view from orbit doesn't just offer scientific advantages for studying Earth. People who have visited space often report that seeing the world in this way leads to a greater appreciation of our extraordinary planet's fragility and isolation in space—a phenomenon known as the Overview Effect.

Shades of green

French astronaut Thomas Pesquet took this picture of the Aube region in northeastern France. It reveals how clearly human activities, such as farming, show from orbit. The land is a patchwork of grain fields, vineyards, and forest.

DID YOU KNOW?

Astronauts can see the outlines of cities from space but not individual buildings.

Red river

This image gives a new viewpoint of an unfolding environmental disaster. Madagascar's Betsiboka River runs red as it gathers silt from the surrounding landscape, where cutting down forests has caused soil to wash away.

Bright city lights

ISS astronauts are treated to spectacular nighttime views too. Despite the surrounding darkness, large cities, such as Shanghai in China, shown here, are still clearly visible from space, thanks to their glistening streetlights.

LIGHT SHOW

From high above Earth, astronauts are lucky to be able to see some of nature's most dazzling events, including spectacular displays of lights called "aurorae." These colorful patterns usually appear at high latitudes around Earth's magnetic north and south poles and look like shimmering curtains of light dancing at the outer edges of the atmosphere.

▶ Glowing aurorae

Energy from the Sun enters, and is stored in, Earth's magnetic field. This energy builds until it is explosively released, accelerating particles toward Earth's magnetic poles, where they bump into gas atoms in the upper atmosphere. These interactions cause bursts of light to be given off, which we see as aurorae.

Solar eclipse

From space, astronauts also get a unique view of rare events, like solar eclipses. These eclipses occur when the Sun, Earth, and Moon line up in such a way that the Moon blocks out the Sun's light, casting a shadow on a section of Earth's surface. If the Sun is only partially blocked, it is called a partial solar eclipse, and if it is fully blocked, it's a total solar eclipse.

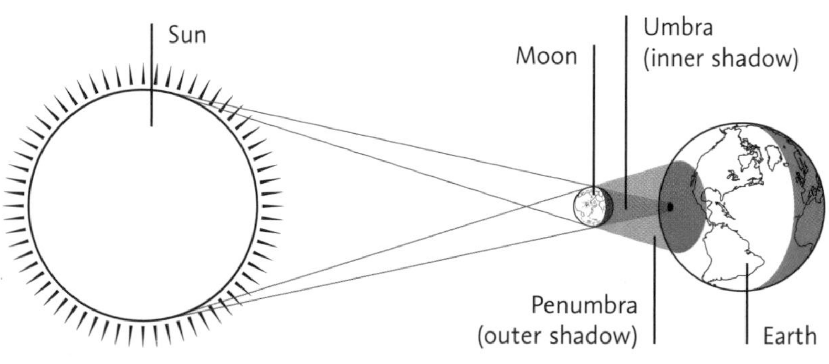

Blotting out the Sun
During an eclipse, astronauts on the ISS see the Moon's shadow appear to race across continents as Earth rotates. The fuzzy outer edge of the shadow, called the penumbra, marks areas where the Sun is only partially blocked.

DID YOU KNOW?

Aurorae—often called the Northern and Southern Lights—can be seen in different colors, such as red, green, purple, and blue.

Astronaut "care package"

After the challenge of successfully docking with a spacecraft full of cargo comes the fun of finding out what's been sent. Along with everyday items, mission planners on Earth make sure there are treats, such as delicious fresh fruit, to keep the astronauts happy.

A friendly face

Robot assistants, such as CIMON (Crew Interactive MObile CompanioN), can provide information to help astronauts with various tasks and even have a friendly, mood-boosting chat with them through the use of artificial intelligence.

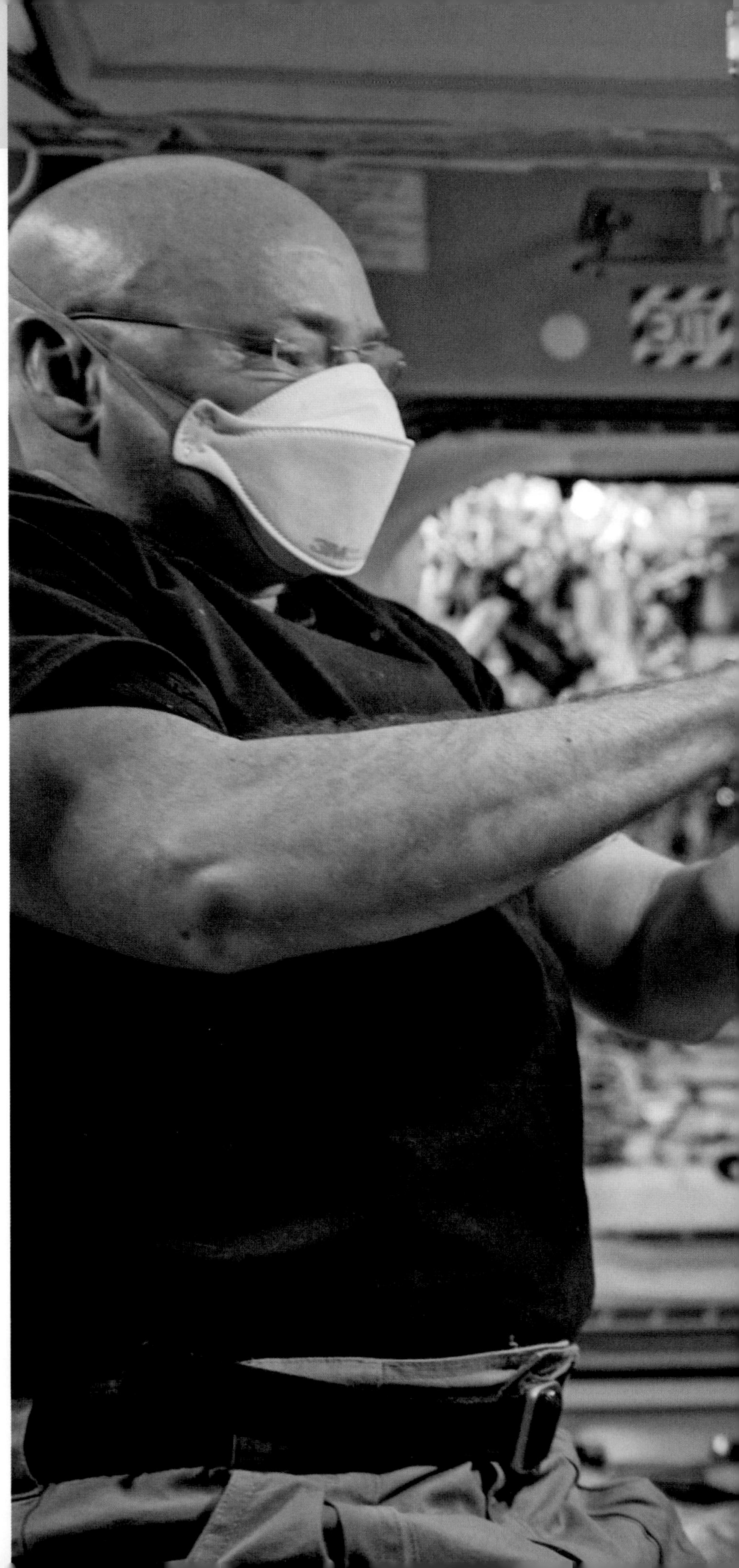

POSITIVE VIBES

During long missions, taking care of astronauts' mental health is just as important as looking after their bodies. Being an astronaut is a demanding, high-pressure job. With no chance of getting away from the other people onboard, it's important that the crew find ways to relax and have fun together on the space station.

◀ Fresh flowers

Growing plants can be as enjoyable and relaxing for astronauts in space as it is for gardeners on Earth. During US astronaut Scott Kelly's yearlong mission on the ISS, he nurtured a crop of zinnia plants to produce bright orange flowers that delighted the entire crew.

BIG MOMENT

Gorilla in space
When US astronaut Scott Kelly's twin bother Mark Kelly sent him a gorilla suit in his birthday "care package," Scott chased his crewmates around the space station at high speed—and captured it all on camera too!

KEEPING FIT

Regular exercise during a long space mission isn't just a luxury, it's a necessity. Life in microgravity causes changes to the body that can leave it less able to function on return to Earth—or even cause issues while an astronaut is still in space. Regular exercise keeps muscles and bones strong and makes the heart work harder to pump blood around the body, but exercise in space brings with it some unique challenges.

▼ Lace up your sneakers

The ISS Treadmill 2 lets astronauts go for a jog in weightless conditions. Before running, they put on a harness that attaches to elasticated straps and helps keep their feet on the base. A vibration isolation system ensures the pounding of footsteps doesn't cause the whole station to shake.

Gripping handles provide the astronaut with more stability.

Snap-on cycling shoes are stored on a shelf behind the exercise bike.

Keep pedaling

The station's exercise bike is known as CEVIS (Cycle Ergometer with Vibration Isolation Stabilization). There's no seat, so astronauts attach themselves to the wall with a belt and clip their shoes into pedals. The base unit can offer different amounts of resistance, mimicking cycling uphill and downhill on Earth.

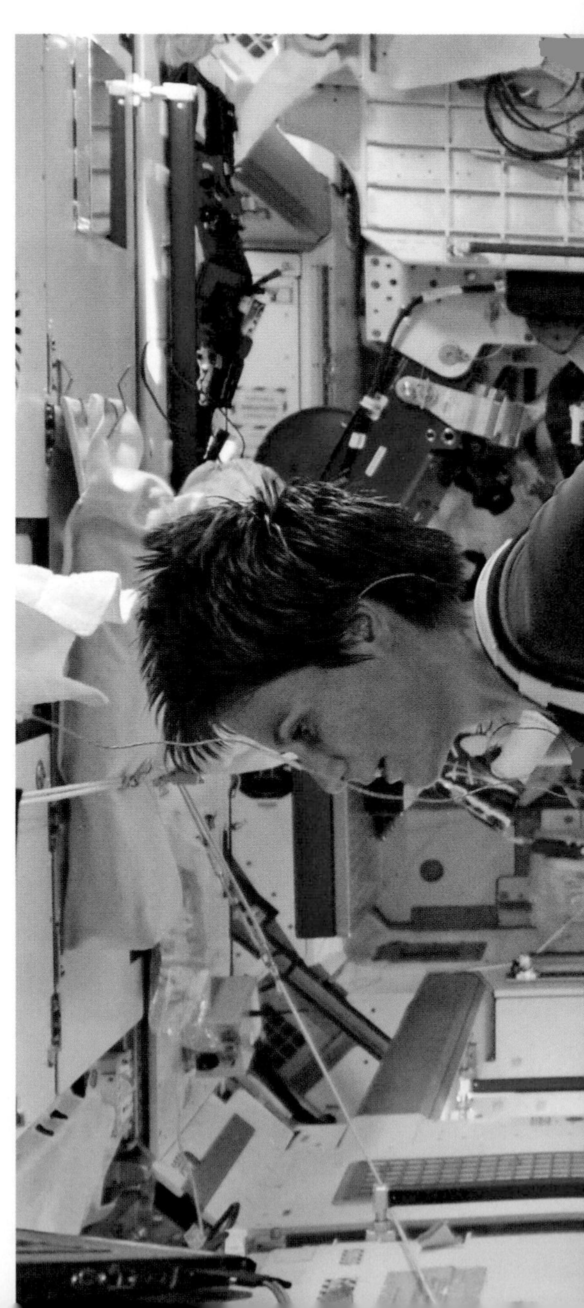

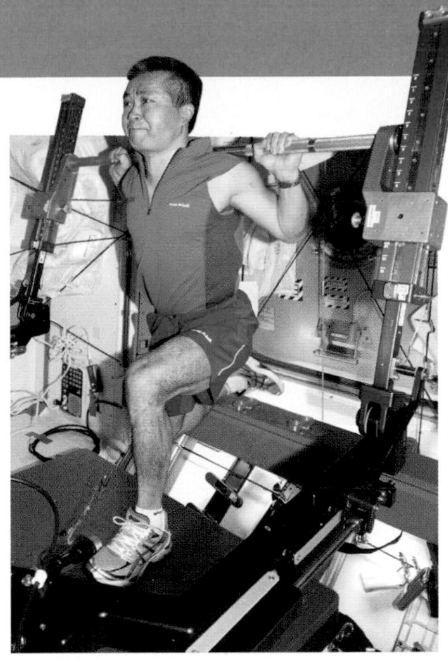

Lifting weights

ARED (Advanced Resistive Exercise Device) uses pistons to simulate lifting weights on Earth. Astronauts can choose between 29 different exercise routines, including squats to strengthen the legs and bicep curls for the upper body.

BIG MOMENT

Marathon record
In April 2016, British astronaut Tim Peake ran the London marathon in space, using the ISS treadmill to complete the 26.2 mile (42.2 km) distance in 3 hours 35 minutes.

TIME OFF

Working on the space station can be tough on both the brain and the body, so the end of each working day includes some time for astronauts to relax before bed. For some, this may simply involve enjoying the view of Earth, but others take their hobbies and pastimes into space.

▶ Stitching in space

US astronaut Karen Nyberg enjoys sewing, so during her 2013 mission, she took along a quilting kit of fabrics, thread, and sewing needles. Even a relaxing hobby like sewing has unique challenges in space, since Nyberg had to stop her fabrics from floating away. "It will be a great experiment controlling everything!" she said before the flight.

Space dino
Nyberg stitched this toy dinosaur for her son with discarded fabric from the lining of Russian food containers.

Quilting together

Using fabric from a discarded spacesuit, Nyberg made the central piece of a star-themed quilt. She invited crafters around the world to design and make their own patches too, which were then stitched into a colorful quilt that was later put on public display.

Hobbies from home

Just like people on Earth, astronauts like to relax in different ways—whether that's finding space for some quiet time, hanging out with their crew mates, or talking to people back on Earth.

Amateur "ham" radio
Alongside official communications equipment, the ISS has an amateur "ham" radio kit. US astronaut Kjell Lindgren (pictured here) is chatting with amateur radio operators on Earth.

Music in space
Several astronauts with musical talents have taken their instruments into space. Here, US astronaut Jessica Meir enjoys playing saxophone in the cupola.

BIG MOMENT

Canadian astronaut Chris Hadfield became an Internet sensation after he performed David Bowie's song "Space Oddity" on guitar while aboard the ISS in 2013.

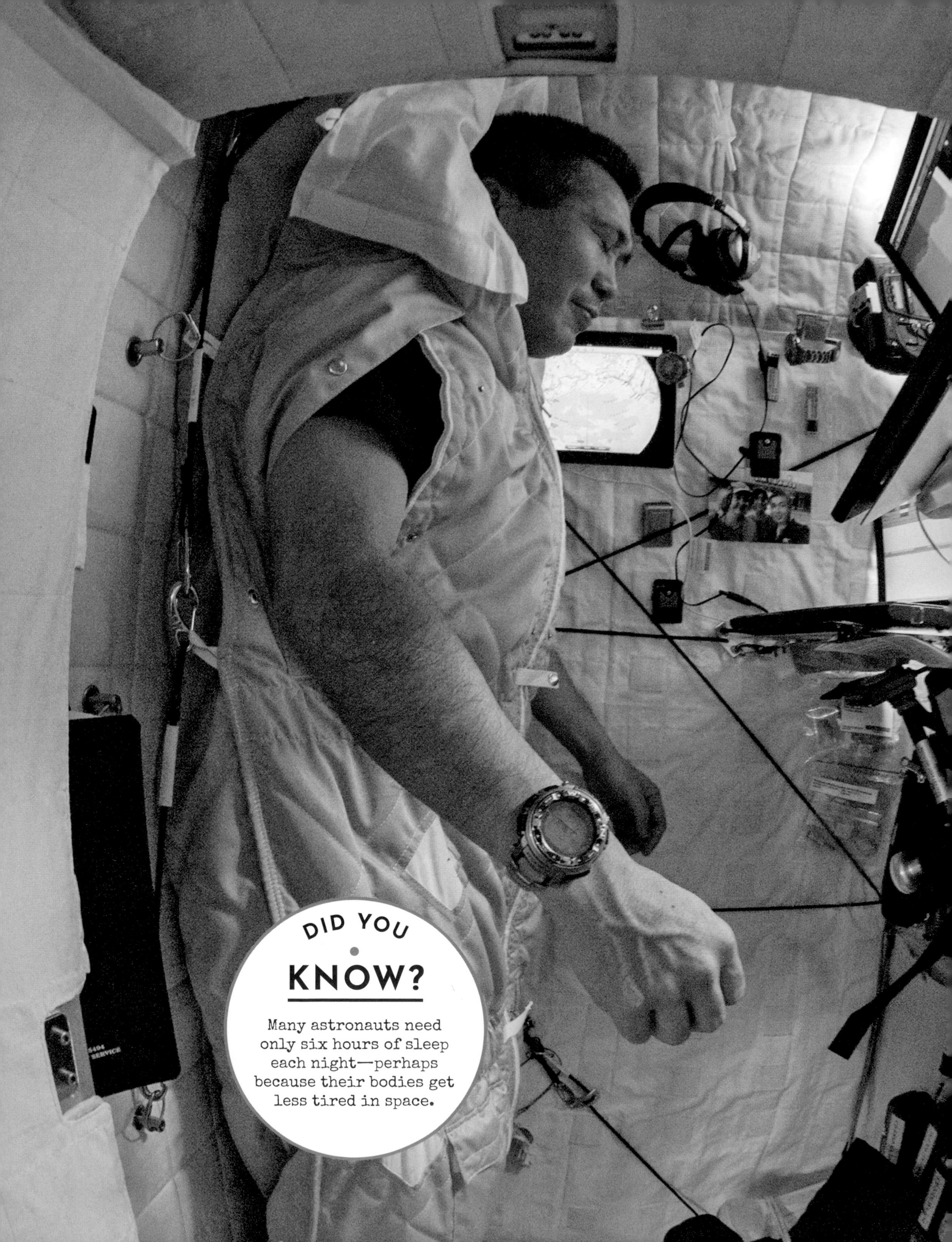

DID YOU KNOW?

Many astronauts need only six hours of sleep each night—perhaps because their bodies get less tired in space.

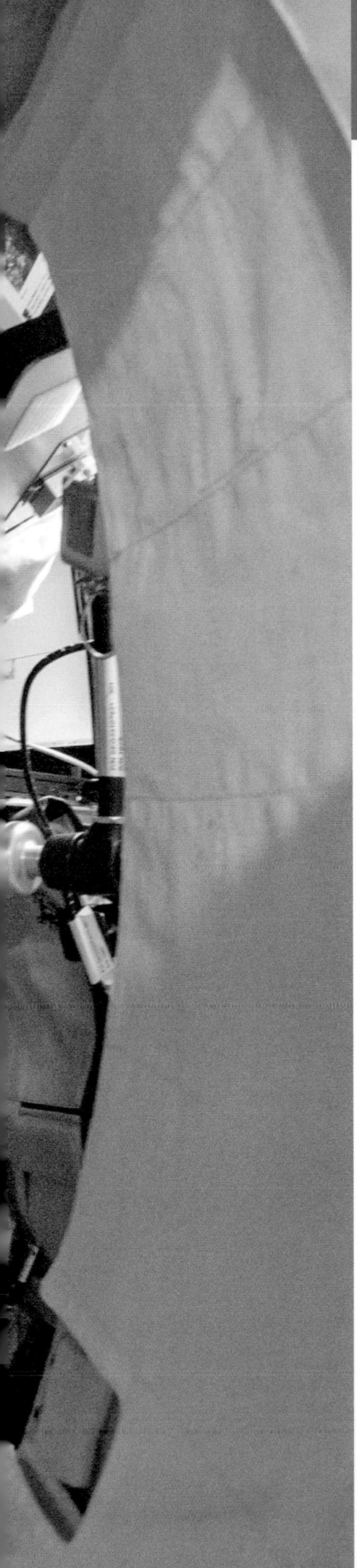

READY FOR BED

During a space station mission, it's vital that astronauts get time to rest and recover, so mission days come to an end with scheduled eight-hour sleep periods. The crew usually all sleep at the same time, often wearing eye masks and earplugs to help cut out the light and noise of the station environment. Meanwhile, mission control keeps constant watch over the station's life-support systems from Earth.

◀ Private quarters

The station usually has seven crew cabins—private quarters about the size of a changing cubicle, with a sleeping bag anchored to one wall, a personal laptop, and room to store a few belongings brought from home. Nearby ventilator fans blow away carbon dioxide breathed out by astronauts; it would otherwise collect around their heads, starving them of oxygen.

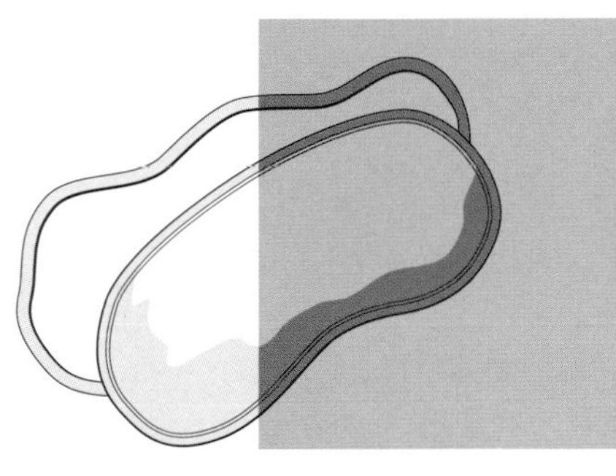

Build a bedroom

During crew changeovers and other busy times, extra crew cabins can be added, but in a pinch, sleeping bags can be attached to almost any flat surface. In 2021, there were briefly 11 people onboard and two astronauts had to sleep in the SpaceX Dragon capsule docked to the station.

Space station at night

Lights on the station are dimmed at night to help the crew's bodies keep in tune with the natural daily rhythms of Earth. But with no strict bedtime, many astronauts enjoy exploring the station at night.

MORNING ROUTINE

When you're living in a tight space with other people for months at a time, personal hygiene is even more important than usual. The ISS provides all the necessary equipment to keep astronauts feeling their best. However, keeping clean in weightless conditions creates challenges—especially when we're so used to water (and other things!) naturally falling downward on Earth.

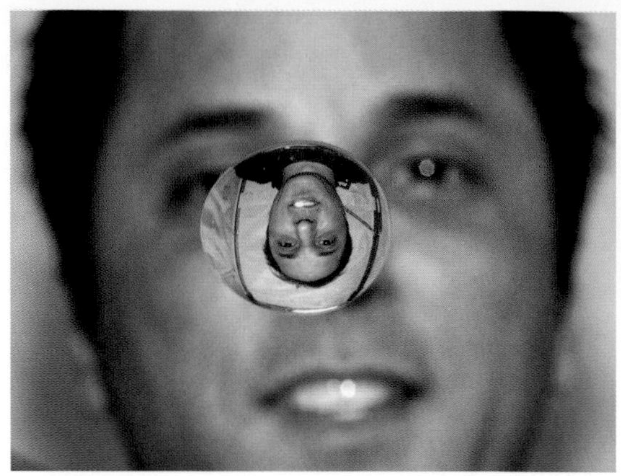

Managing water in space

On Earth, the force of gravity pulls water downward. Inside the space station, however, microgravity conditions allow water to float freely, and surface tension (a weak force that pulls the surface inward) creates spherical droplets like this one.

Microgravity wash

Weightless conditions in space make it hard to enjoy an effective shower, so instead, astronauts bathe with liquid soap and warmed water squeezed onto their skin from pouches. They dry with a towel, while a high-powered fan catches any water droplets in the air to be recycled.

Washing hair
Astronauts with longer hair can use rinseless shampoo that removes dirt and grease from hair without the need for much water. They use pouches of water to dampen their hair, squirt in the shampoo, and then clean and dry with a towel.

Regular haircuts
Many astronauts prefer to keep their hair short in space. They use an electric razor with a vacuum attachment to suck up trimmed hairs before they float away.

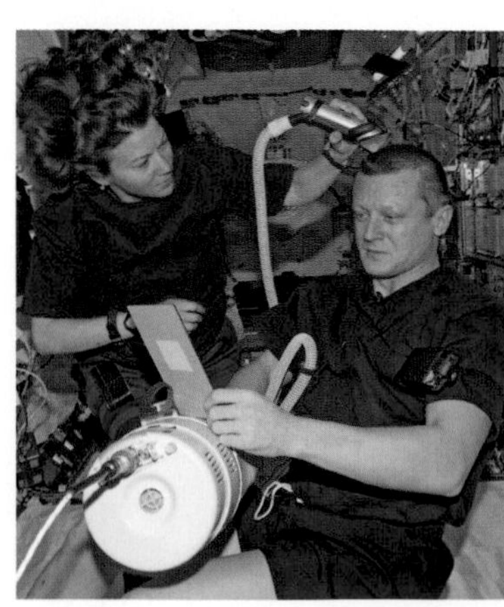

DID YOU KNOW?

You can't wash clothes in space, so astronauts wear the same outfits for as long as possible, then throw them away.

Brushing teeth

Station crew keep their teeth clean in more or less the same way as on Earth—the main challenge is getting a blob of water into the brush at the beginning. With nowhere to spit after brushing, the solution is just to swallow it down.

Astronauts' hygiene kits are strapped to the wall in the washing area.

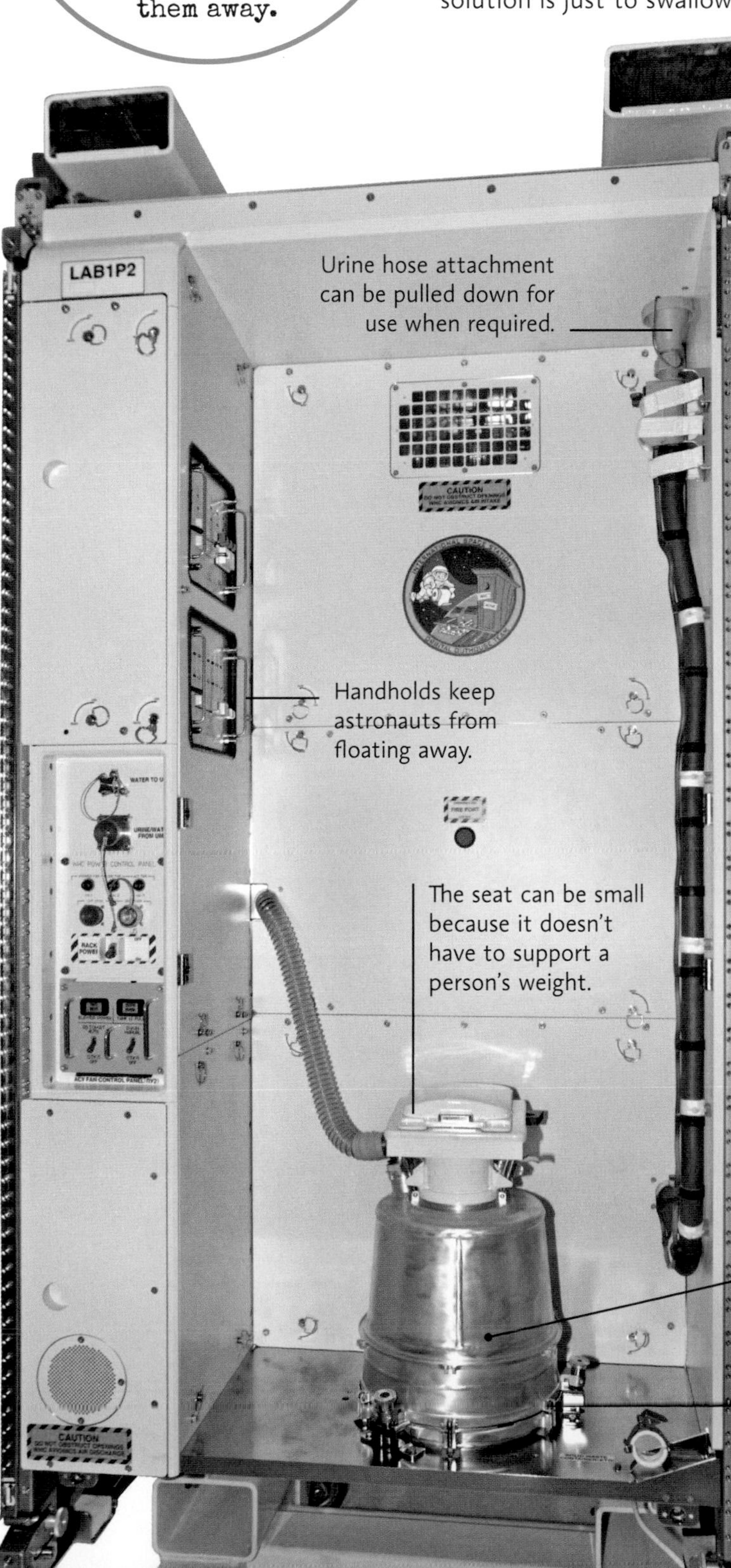

Urine hose attachment can be pulled down for use when required.

Handholds keep astronauts from floating away.

The seat can be small because it doesn't have to support a person's weight.

Air current pulls solid waste into a removable canister.

◀ Space toilet

Going to the bathroom is tricky in space. The ISS has three toilets on board, the latest of which arrived in 2020. Each one uses the flow of air to make sure everything goes in the right direction and is located inside a private cubicle. Treated urine is passed into the station's water recycling system to extract water, while solid waste is dealt with separately.

Urine funnel
Both male and female astronauts pee into a hose that has a funnel-shaped attachment. A fan inside sucks urine through the funnel into the station's water recycling system. The funnel can be removed for cleaning.

Vital maintenance
Solid waste is compacted and stored in a removable canister before being either returned to Earth or loaded onto a cargo vehicle bound to burn-up in Earth's atmosphere.

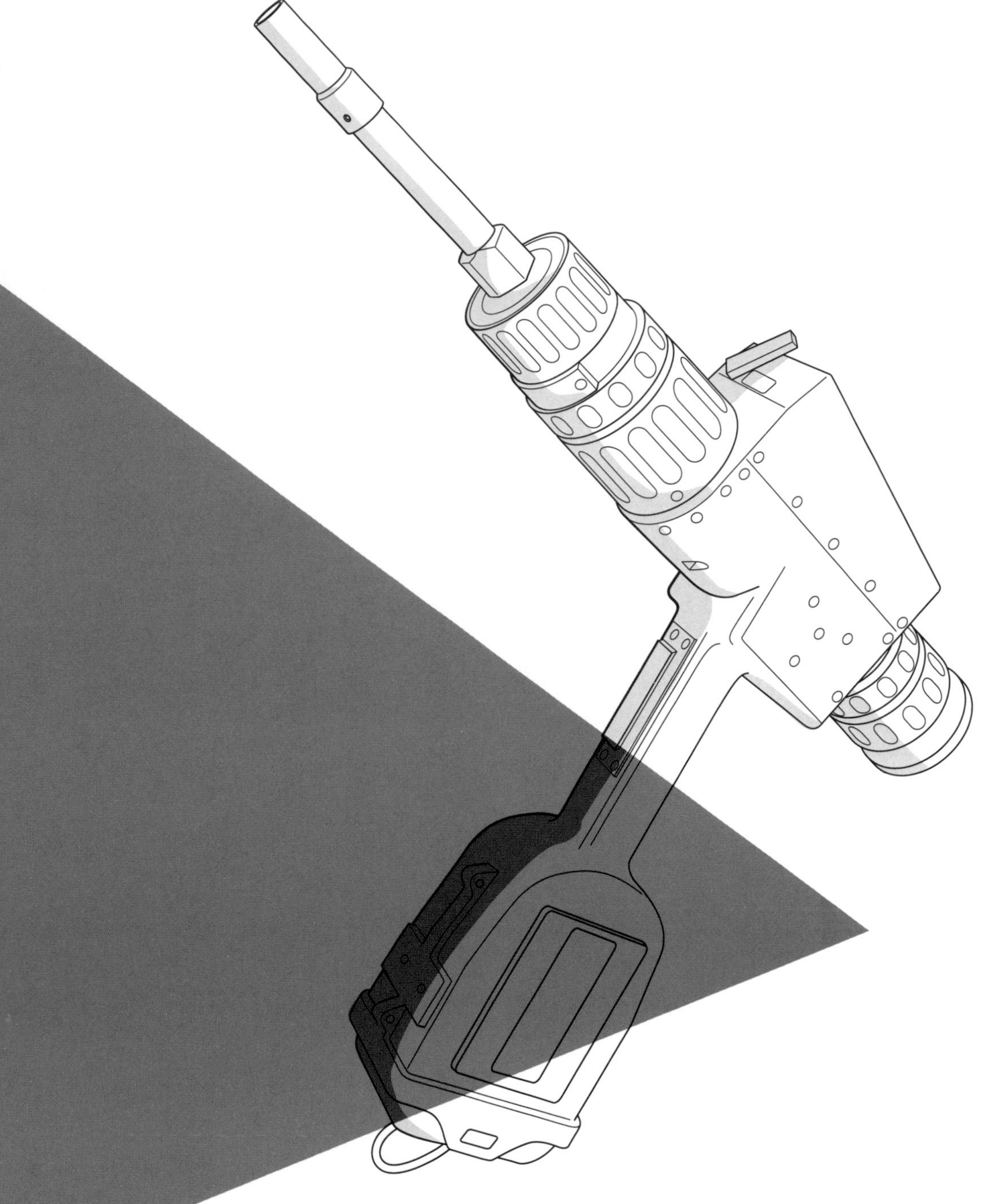

ASTRONAUTS AT WORK

The ISS is a huge science laboratory in orbit, and the crew looks after an enormous range of experiments—sometimes even using themselves as test subjects. So far, more than 3,000 experiments have been carried out on the space station. All this research helps scientists back on Earth find ways to make life in space safer for astronauts and benefit humanity, too, with medical discoveries and new inventions. Some experiments even take place outside the space station, in the extreme conditions of space. Checking on these—and carrying out any important station maintenance—involves the most thrilling part of any space mission: a spacewalk.

SCIENCE LABS

Performing science experiments is one of the crew's most important jobs. To help them produce accurate results, astronauts are taught essential scientific skills before their mission, and they receive lots of guidance from specialists on Earth too. NASA, Roscosmos, JAXA, and ESA each have their own dedicated laboratory modules, but almost any area of the station can be used for experiments.

Inside the LSG
The Life Sciences Glovebox (LSG) is a sealed unit in the Japanese *Kibo* module. Using special gloves, astronauts carry out experiments here without the risk of contamination.

◀ Medical research

Astronauts carry out medical experiments on the space station in order to understand the impact of space travel on human health. Here, US astronaut and microbiologist Kate Rubins investigates the way heart cells adjust to microgravity inside the LSG.

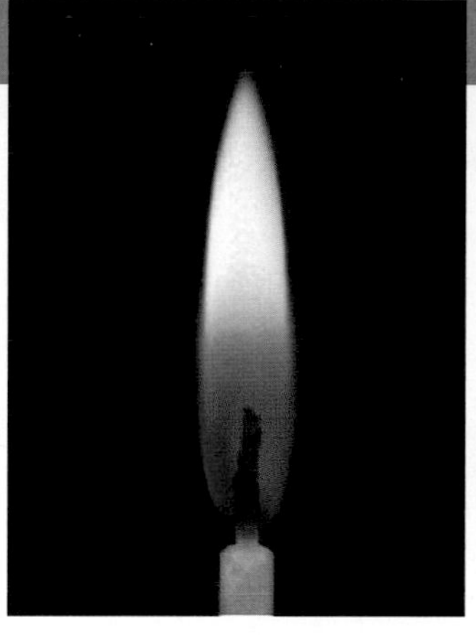

EARTH

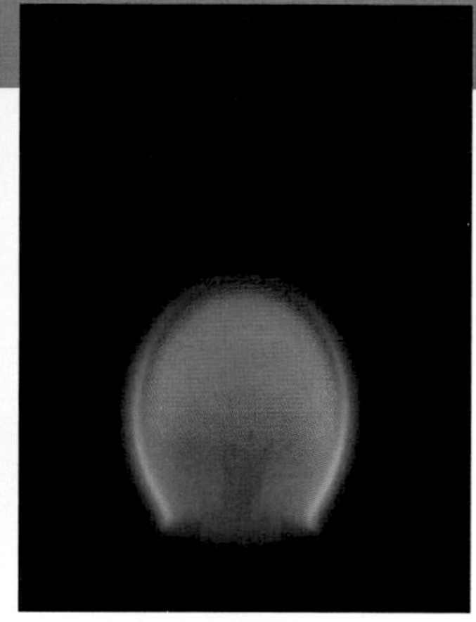

SPACE

Fire experiments

On Earth, flames flicker upward as they burn because the gases inside them expand with heat and become lighter, making them rise. In space, however, a flame burns in a ball shape because the gases simply expand outward without rising. Understanding how fire behaves in space could help scientists design more efficient engines.

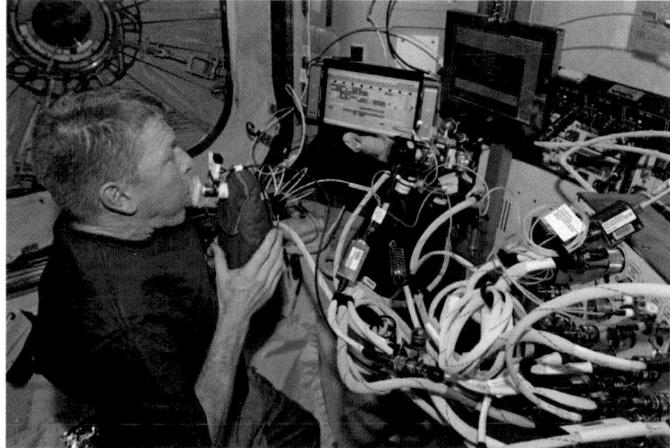

Weightless guinea pigs

Being weightless affects the body—astronauts' bones and muscles get weaker the longer they stay in space. It's similar to the bone and muscle loss experienced by elderly people on Earth. By doing tests on themselves, astronauts can help scientists find new treatments.

MELFI freezers

Sometimes it's necessary to store the results of biology experiments for a long time before they can be transported back to an Earth-based laboratory for analysis. ESA's MELFI (Minus Eighty-degree Laboratory Freezer for ISS) helps keep them fresh.

Animals on the ISS

The station's human crew are often joined by other live creatures. Taking animals into space gives scientists the opportunity to study how their behavior and biology change in microgravity.

Medaka fish
The bones of medaka fish weaken quickly in space. Their see-through bodies make it possible to see this change as it happens.

Golden orb spider
These spiders showed that in microgravity conditions, they use light to orientate themselves in order to build webs.

Bobtail squid
This tiny squid has an immune system similar to a human's. Understanding it could help prevent astronauts getting sick on long missions.

CHANGING BODIES

Spending a long time being weightless can be really bad for astronauts' bodies. Keeping track of any physical changes helps doctors on the ground monitor the health of the onboard crew and also allows them to come up with new ways to keep future astronauts physically fit on missions farther from Earth.

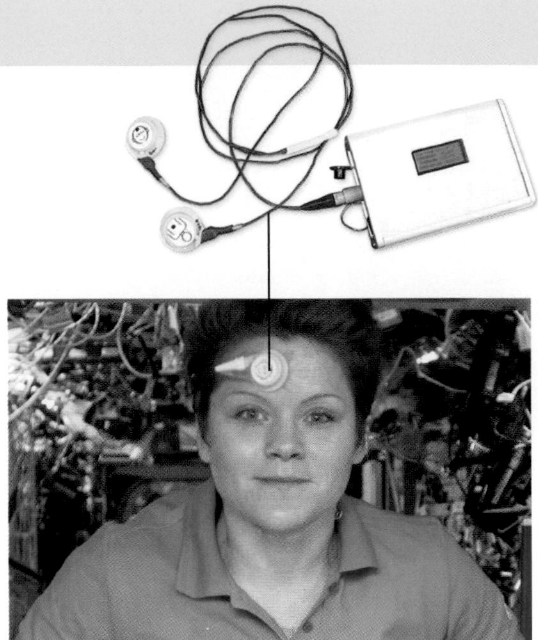

Out of sync

We all have hormones, chemical messengers in the body, that tell us when to sleep and when to wake up, but the bright lights of the ISS and not being able to lie down in space can disrupt the body's natural rhythms. Scientists study these changes by attaching special sensors to astronauts' foreheads.

BIG MOMENT

Identical twins study
As part of a unique experiment, US astronaut Scott Kelly stayed on the ISS for a year while his identical twin brother and fellow astronaut Mark Kelly remained on Earth. By studying twins, scientists were able to learn a lot about how living in space for a long time can affect the body.

▶ Blurred vision

When in weightless conditions, blood and other fluids in an astronaut's body collect in different places, including in the head. As well as making their faces puffy, this puts pressure on their brains, which in turn puts pressure on and can distort the shape of their eyes, weakening their eyesight. Here, US astronaut Karen Nyberg performs an eye test on herself to learn more about this physical change.

Tech help

Scientists and engineers have come up with new technologies to help them learn more about the dangers of space travel and to reverse some of the physical effects of living in microgravity.

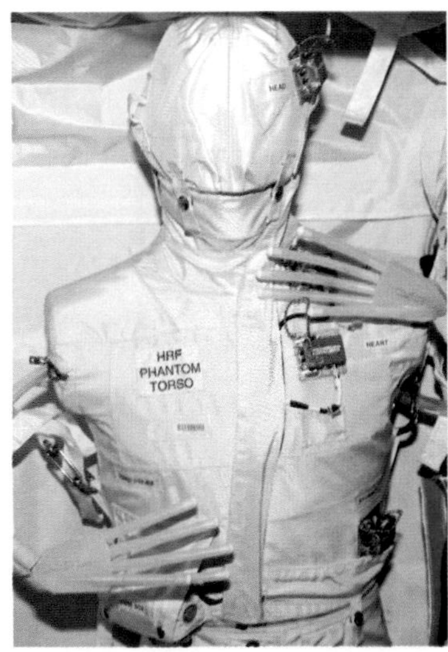

Radiation risk
Astronauts are exposed to cosmic radiation in space—high-energy particles released by the Sun and other stars, which can be harmful to the body. Sensors in this "phantom torso" monitor radiation levels.

Microgravity trousers
The Russian Space Agency's "Chibis" suit is an odd-looking pair of trousers that uses suction, like a vacuum cleaner, to force fluids to move away from the head toward the lower body.

DID YOU
KNOW?
Astronauts often have to wear glasses for a while after they return to Earth. Their eyesight may even be changed permanently.

SPACE GARDEN

A space station might not seem like the ideal environment for growing plants, but that's just what some ISS experiments involve. These experiments help astronauts and scientists practice growing fruits and vegetables in space. Fresh produce is a vital part of a healthy diet, and astronauts on future missions to the Moon or Mars will need to grow their own, as they won't be able to receive fresh supplies from Earth.

▼ Plant power

Gardening in space presents many challenges, although several plants have been successfully grown, including those below. In space, water doesn't drain away from roots like it does on Earth, so astronauts have to make sure that their plants get the water they need without becoming waterlogged.

Gardening equipment

The Vegetable Production System, called Veggie, is used to produce a range of crops. Seeds are planted in "pillows" rather than soil, and LED lights are adjusted to vary growing conditions. Experiments have shown that using specific colors of light can affect the balance of nutrients in crops, potentially creating superfoods.

The "outredgeous" red romaine lettuce was the first salad crop eaten in space.

"Bright lights" Swiss chard is rich in vitamin K.

Chilies in space

In 2021, the crew aboard the ISS planted the first batch of chili peppers in space. As well as providing nutrition, the fresh chilies could, on long missions, add some spice to their diets. The bright colors of the chilies are thought to be good for the astronauts' mental health too.

1 Researchers on Earth used replicas of ISS equipment to test and select the most suitable chili types for space.

2 The chili seeds were delivered to the ISS by rocket. An astronaut set them up in the Veggie box.

3 The chilies were grown in the sealed box in which water, light, and temperature were automatically controlled.

4 Four months after they were planted, the chilies were ready to harvest. The astronauts ate them in tacos!

Plant pillows

The Veggie system can hold six "pillows," each of which produces one plant. The pillows contain a clay-based substance and fertilizer. They allow just the right balance of water, nutrients, and air to circulate around each plant's roots.

"Sugar Pod II" snow peas produce a harvest that can be used to plant new crops.

Paintbrush pollination

Pollen is a fine powder that plants create to help them reproduce. As there are no insects on the ISS to transfer pollen between flowers, astronauts use a paintbrush to collect pollen from the anthers (male parts) of one flower and transfer it onto the stigma (female part) of another.

The "Cherry bomb hybrid II" variety of radish has edible leaves and roots.

"Tokyo Bekana" is a Chinese cabbage chosen for its small size and fast growth.

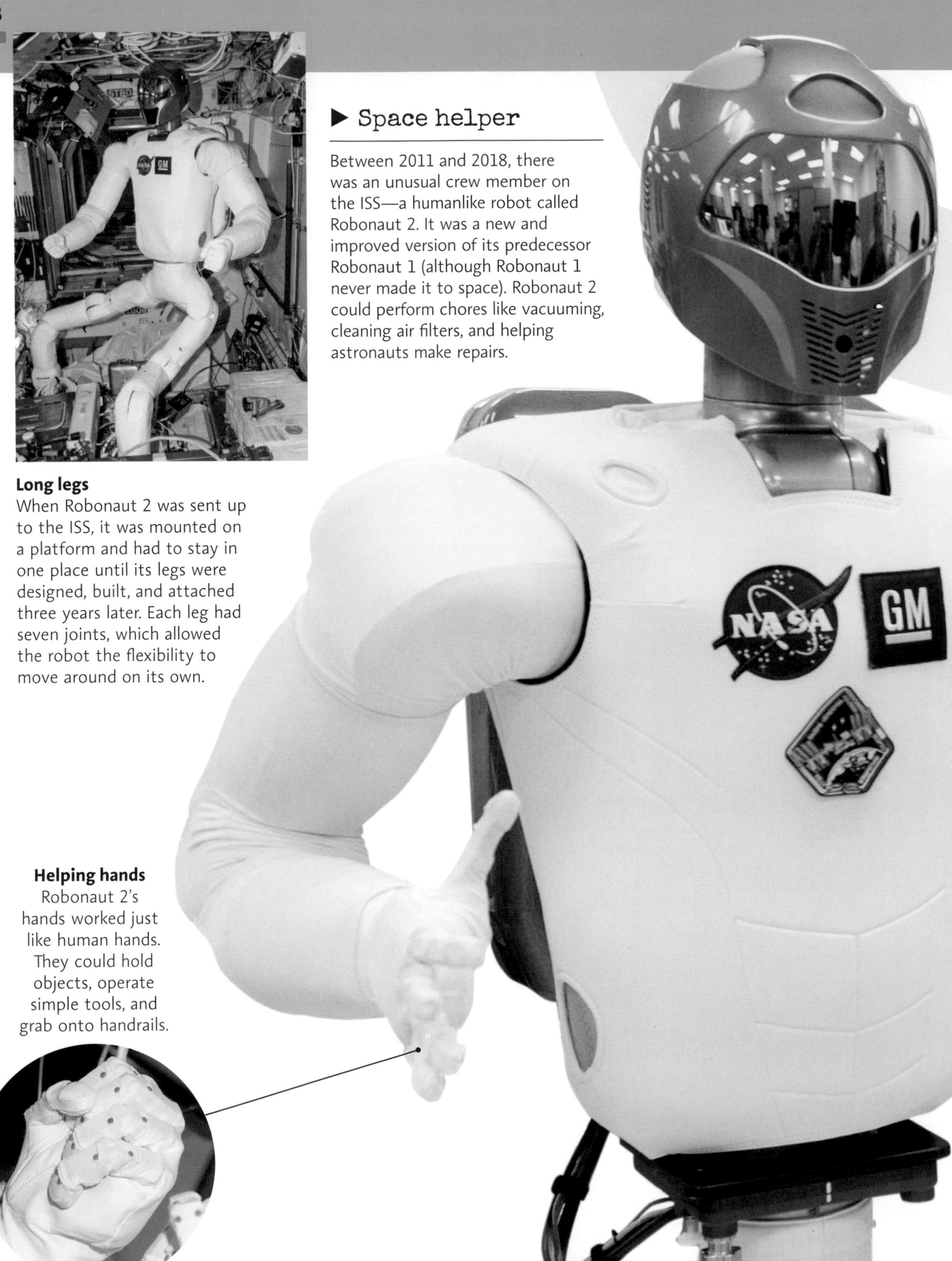

▶ Space helper

Between 2011 and 2018, there was an unusual crew member on the ISS—a humanlike robot called Robonaut 2. It was a new and improved version of its predecessor Robonaut 1 (although Robonaut 1 never made it to space). Robonaut 2 could perform chores like vacuuming, cleaning air filters, and helping astronauts make repairs.

Long legs
When Robonaut 2 was sent up to the ISS, it was mounted on a platform and had to stay in one place until its legs were designed, built, and attached three years later. Each leg had seven joints, which allowed the robot the flexibility to move around on its own.

Helping hands
Robonaut 2's hands worked just like human hands. They could hold objects, operate simple tools, and grab onto handrails.

SPACE ROBOTS

Living in space is exciting, but it's also hard work. Just like us on Earth, astronauts sometimes need help. As robots don't get tired, don't need a lunch break, and never get bored, they are used onboard the space station to support astronauts with some of their time-consuming or less interesting tasks.

Int-Ball

As big as a grapefruit, the Int-Ball, launched by the Japanese Space Agency JAXA in 2017, helps astronauts record videos and take photographs of their activities—tasks that often take up a lot of time.

The round, blue "eyes" light up when the Int-Ball is in use.

Smart ball
Floating in microgravity, the Int-Ball moves itself around using its 12 tiny electric fans. An onboard camera and sensors help prevent it from bumping into things.

Space photographer
The Int-Ball can record videos while being controlled by the JAXA mission control on Earth. Its glowing eyes indicate which way its camera is facing.

Astrobees

The Astrobees are three robotic assistants named Bumble, Honey, and Queen. They were designed by NASA to help save astronauts time by taking care of everyday tasks, such as filming experiments, monitoring sound levels and air quality, and alerting astronauts to lost items blocking air vents.

The blue lights signal that the robot is now "listening" for the astronauts' commands.

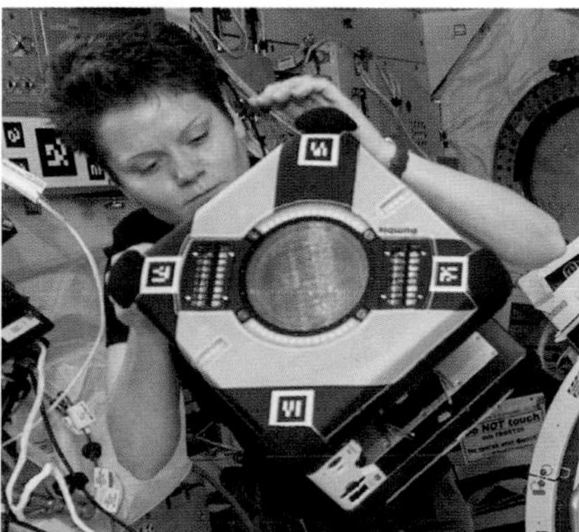

Extra help
US astronaut Anne McClain unpacked Bumble in Japan's *Kibo* module in April 2019. Bumble was the first of the three Astrobees to be delivered. It can be controlled by astronauts or by staff back on Earth.

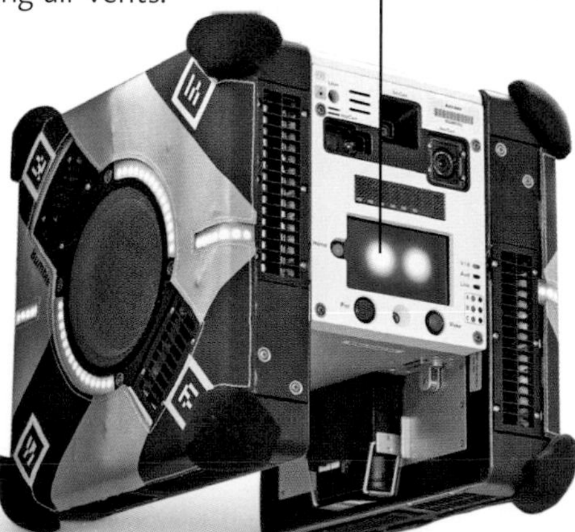

Efficient assistant
Propelled by electric fans, the cube-shaped Bumble has cameras and sensors to avoid collisions. When its batteries are almost empty, it returns to its docking station to recharge. Each Astrobee is activated when an astronaut calls out its name.

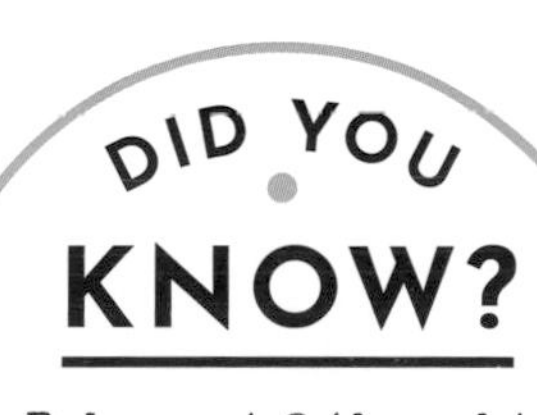

DID YOU KNOW?

Robonaut 2 thought with its "stomach"—where its computers were located.

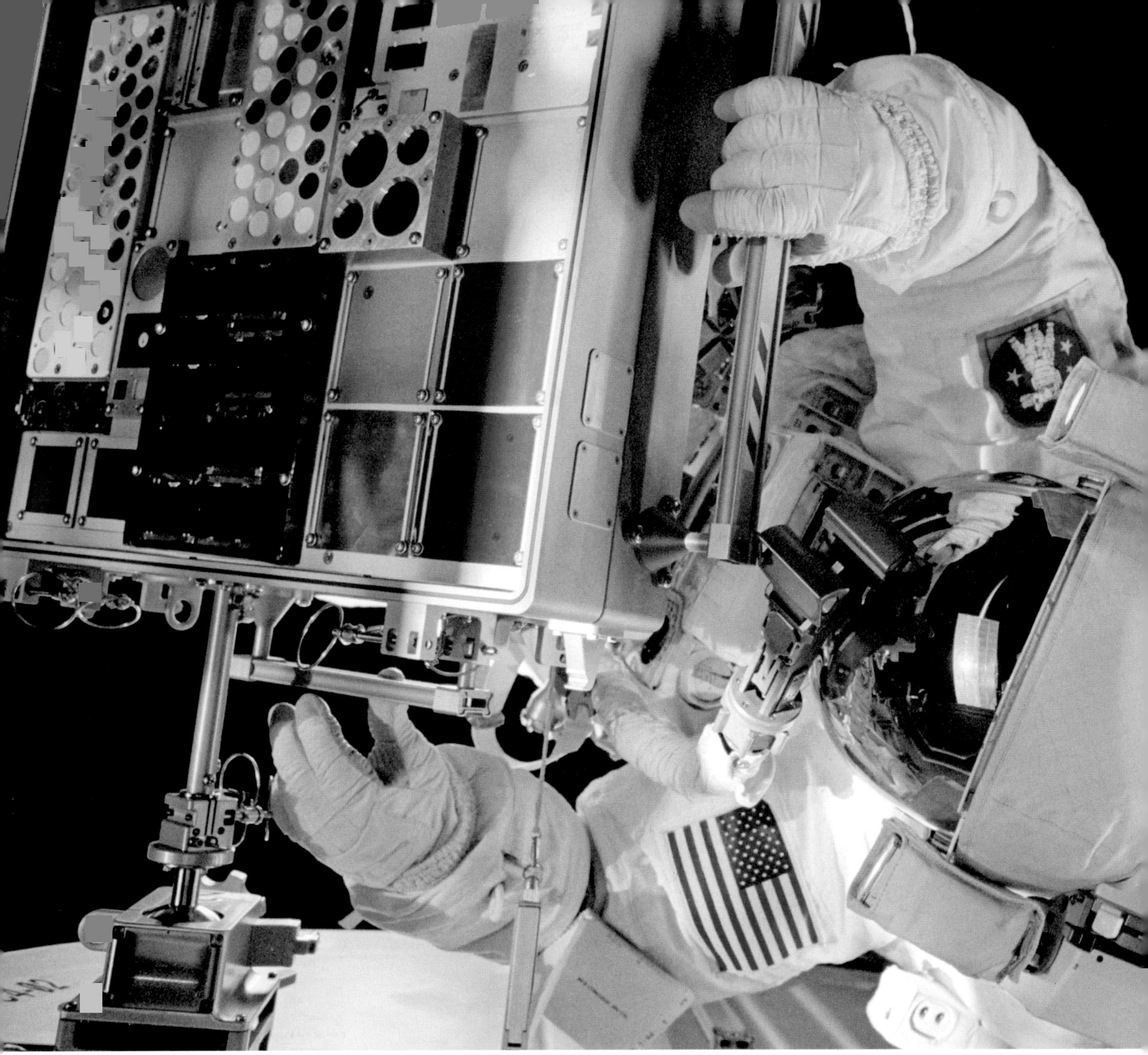

Tiny satellites

Recent advances in electronics have allowed engineers to build increasingly small satellites, some so tiny you could fit them in your hand. Weighing as little as 2 lb (1 kg), these "nanosatellites" can perform the same tasks as traditional, large satellites, but they cost far less to build and launch. Nanosatellites can be flown to the ISS and launched from there.

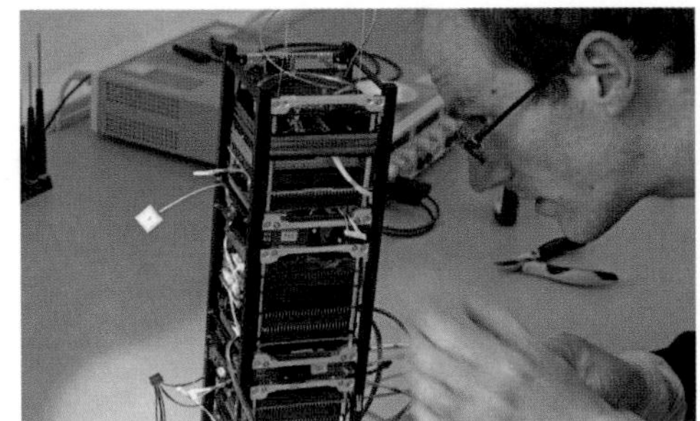

New technology
This shoebox-sized nanosatellite, called GomX-3, took just a year to develop. It has technology onboard that can detect aircraft signals.

Launchpad in space
Nanosatellites are launched from Japan's *Kibo* module into new orbits at a safe distance from the station. It's cheaper than launching them from Earth.

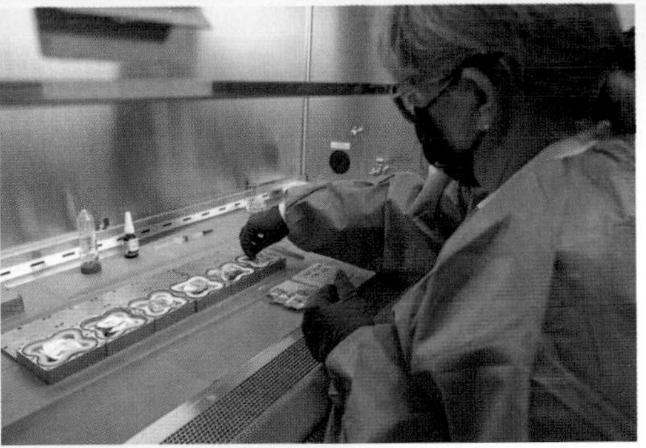

Preparing seeds for space
Astronauts on longer missions to the Moon or Mars will need to grow plants for food, so it's vital we understand how seeds cope with conditions in space. Here, a scientist prepares seeds for an experiment outside the ISS.

◀ Outside experiments

Objects exposed to space experience an almost perfect vacuum (a space with no material of any kind), extremes of heat and cold, and bombardment with cosmic radiation. To understand how vital space equipment, such as heat shields and solar panels, is affected by these conditions, several palettes like this one, full of samples, have been mounted on the station exterior for months or even years.

SCIENCE OUTDOORS

As well as performing experiments inside the space station, astronauts sometimes head outside to do experiments there. These outdoor experiments help scientists on Earth learn more about how different materials, substances, and even some of Earth's life-forms react to the extreme conditions of space. When an experiment is complete, samples can be returned to Earth for detailed analysis.

Space survivors

Experiments on the station have shown that, surprisingly, some of Earth's life-forms are able to handle the hostile conditions of space. Understanding how these creatures survive and adapt may provide clues to protect future astronauts on long-duration spaceflights.

Tardigrade
Despite being just a couple of millimeters long, tiny tardigrades can survive almost anything, including blasts of intense cosmic radiation, extremes of hot and cold, and even exposure to the vacuum of space.

Hardy bacteria
Deinococcus radiodurans is a radiation-resistant bacterium that has survived in space and could thrive on the surface of Mars. So, future missions to Mars should take care not to contaminate the Red Planet with bacteria from Earth.

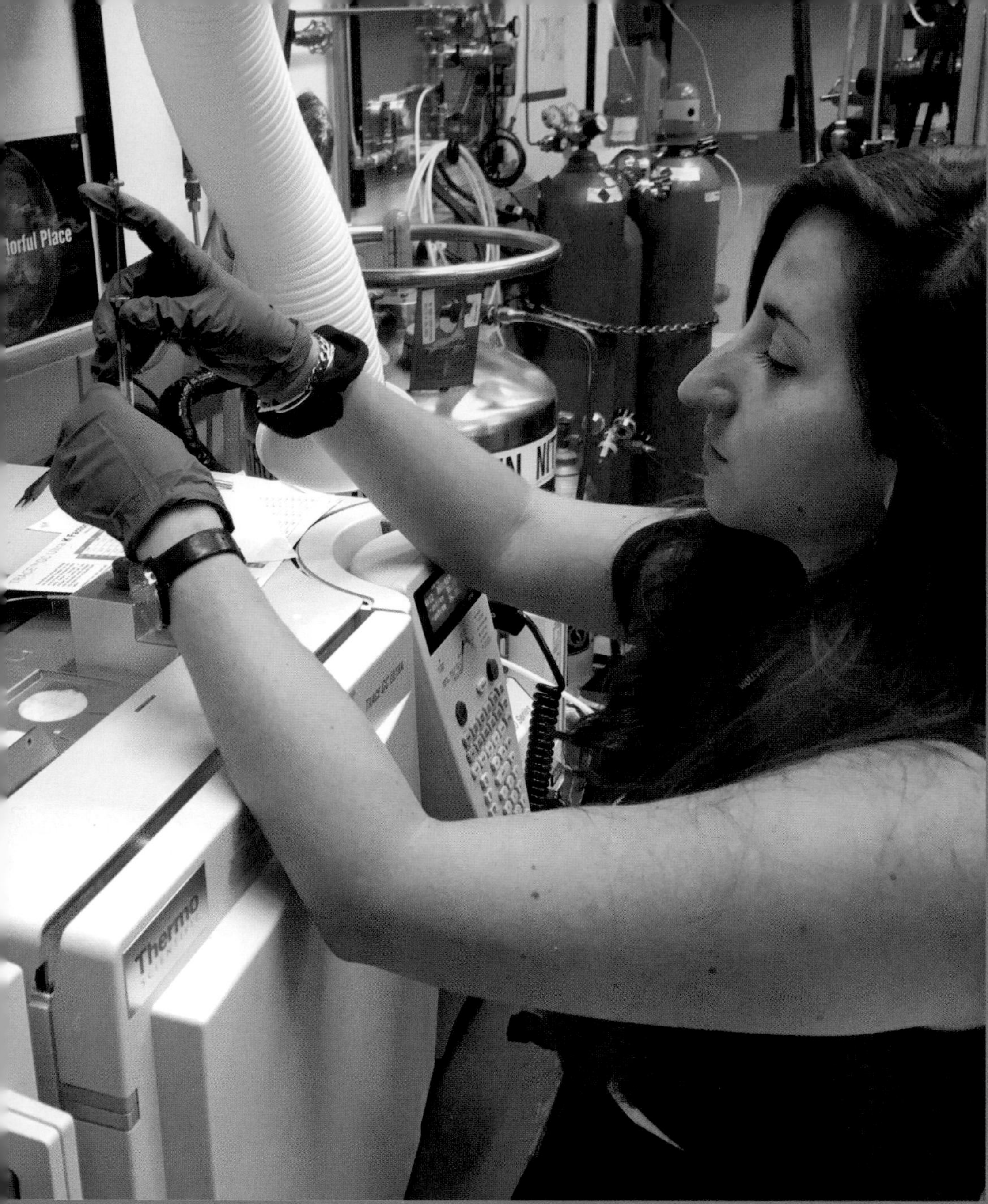

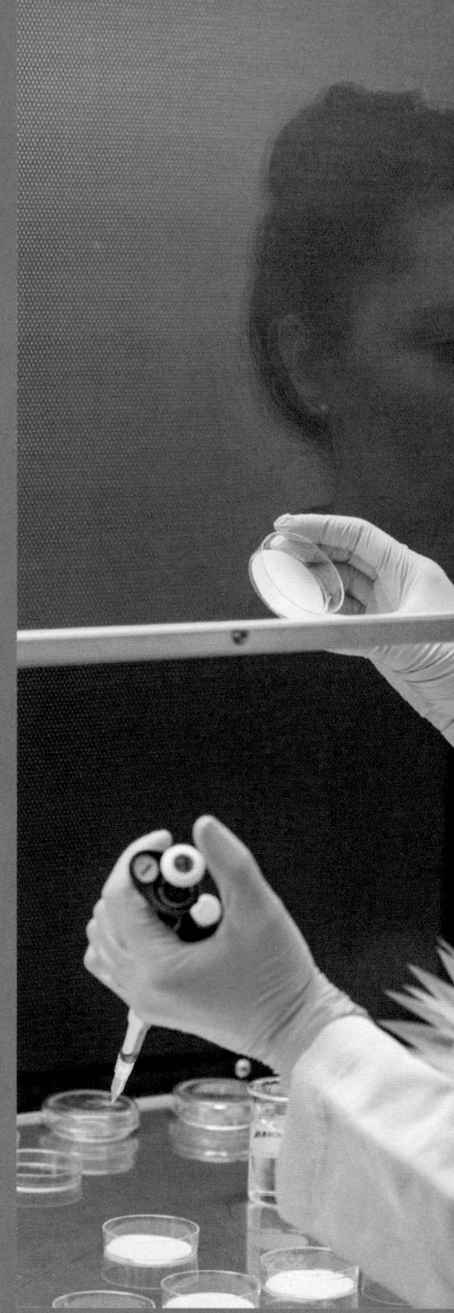

ROLES BEHIND THE SCENES

SCIENTIST

Thousands of scientists are employed by or work with space agencies. They are specialists in many subjects, from biochemistry to astrophysics, and they use their skills, knowledge, and research to help advance humanity's understanding of space. They make exciting discoveries that reveal how our planet and the universe work. Scientists on the ground also provide invaluable support to crews during a mission by preparing experiments to be flown into space, helping astronauts carry them out, then analyzing the data once they've been completed.

Out in the field

Some experiments may take scientists out of the lab—for example, to use equipment like these huge radar dishes near Longyearbyen, Svalbard, Norway. They help gather data about the aurora, space weather, and space debris.

Wide knowledge base ▲
Scientists employed in space research have a wide range of expertise—shown here are specialists in astrobiology, planetary science, and plant science.

Experiment preparation

Here, scientists at the NASA Ames Research Center in California are preparing fruit flies to be sent into space to support research into the effects of microgravity on the human heart and blood vessels. Since the ISS first began operations, more than 3,000 experiments have been carried out there.

SPACEWALK PREP

Preparations for a spacewalk, called an Extra-Vehicular Activity (EVA), can begin up to a year in advance. It's a team effort, with astronauts, scientists, engineers, and mission control all involved. About two weeks before the date of the planned EVA, the crew begin spending two to three hours a day carrying out checks, called the "Road to EVA."

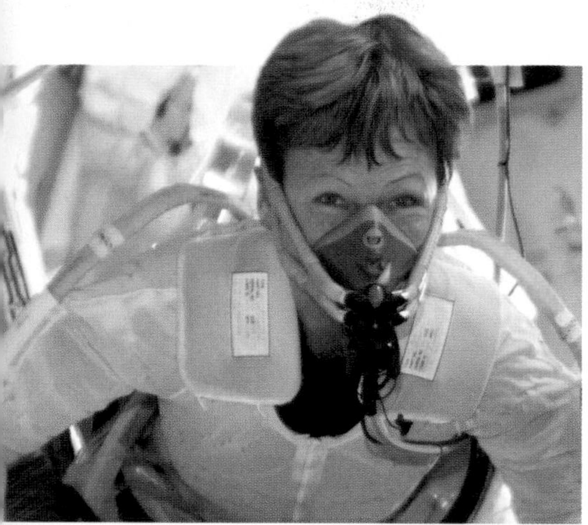

Pure oxygen

In the hours before and then during their EVA, an astronaut must breathe pure oxygen to remove nitrogen from the blood. If they don't, painful gas bubbles could start to form in the body while they are outside—a condition known as "the bends."

▶ Suiting up

Astronauts always perform spacewalks in pairs, supported by a third crew member inside the ISS. Here, Japanese astronaut Soichi Noguchi (center) is shown assisting US astronauts Victor Glover (left) and Kate Rubins (right) before an EVA in 2021. Following countless safety checks, the astronauts close the inner hatch of the airlock behind them, shutting it tight. Air is then gradually pumped out of the airlock. When there is no air left, the outer hatch—the door to space—is opened, and the astronauts float out.

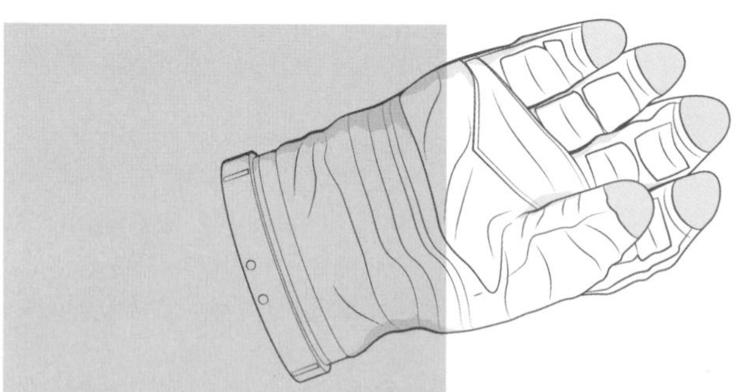

DID YOU KNOW?

Spacewalking astronauts cannot use deodorant, as it poses a fire risk when mixed with the pure oxygen atmosphere in their suits.

3015

SPACESUIT READY

The spacesuits that astronauts use for spacewalks are different than those worn during launch and landing. Outside the ISS, astronauts face many dangers, from space debris to extreme temperatures. Their spacesuits must act like personal spacecraft and supply the wearer with everything needed to stay alive and work safely in space.

▶ US spacesuit

NASA's spacesuit, formed of 14 different layers of material, is called the Extra-Vehicular Mobility Unit (EMU). It has two parts that seal together—a rigid top half that goes over the head and a more flexible bottom half that is put on like pants. The helmet and gloves are attached separately.

The fingertips of the thick gloves are made with silicone rubber to increase touch sensitivity.

Colored stripes help onlookers tell one astronaut from another.

The "feet" of the spacesuit are made from a soft material to prevent any damage to the space station's exterior.

Russian Orlan spacesuit

Russia's Orlan spacesuit has been in use since the 1970s, with just a few updates. Unlike NASA's EMU, the Orlan (meaning "eagle") is a one-piece spacesuit; the wearer steps into it through a hatch at the back, which is then sealed.

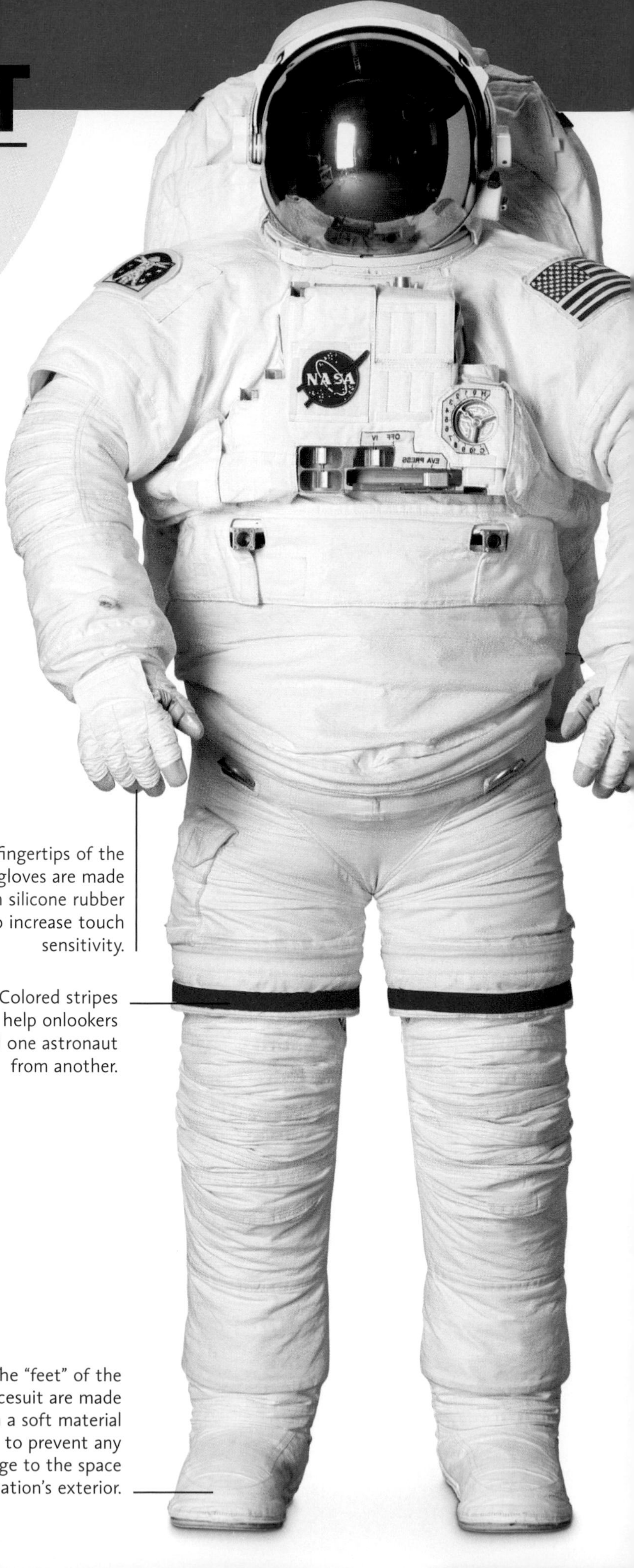

Dressing for space

In addition to their spacesuit, spacewalking astronauts need a few essential pieces of equipment to keep them safe and comfortable.

Constant temperature
Warm or cool water is pumped through a network of tubes in this stretchy undergarment, worn beneath the spacesuit, to keep astronauts at a comfortable temperature while they work.

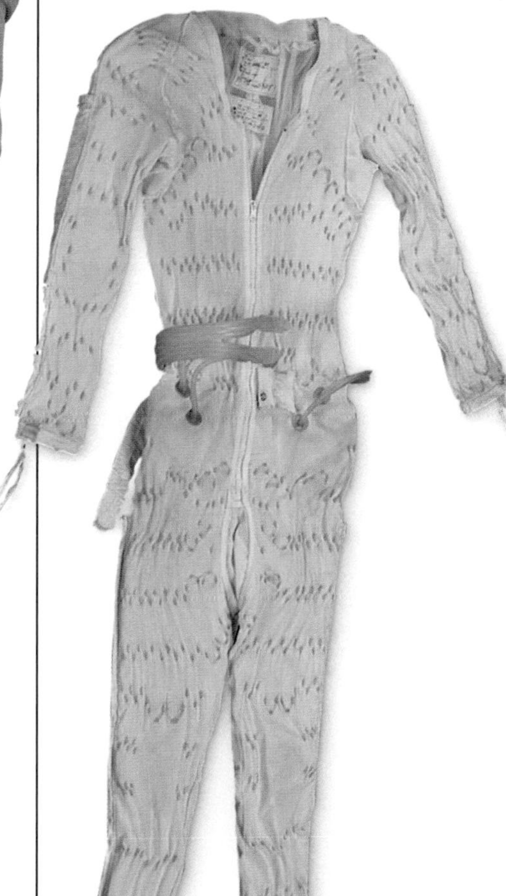

The soft undergarment contains 300 ft (90 m) of tubing.

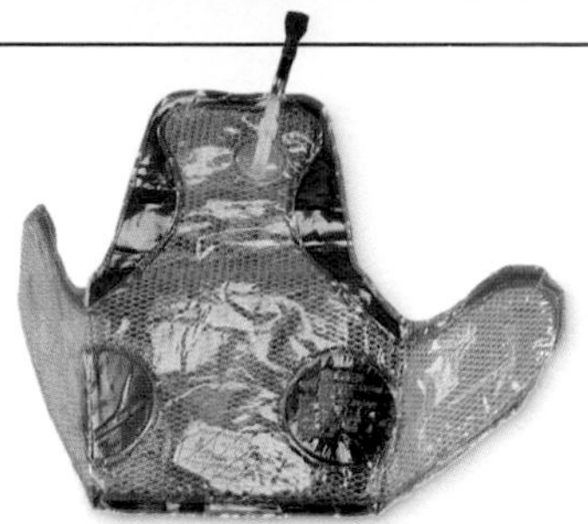

Staying hydrated
This hydration pack attaches inside the suit's torso. It releases water when the plastic straw is bitten.

Life-support backpack
Mounted inside the suit's backpack, the Primary Life Support System (PLSS) contains oxygen and water tanks, batteries for power, and a radio for communication.

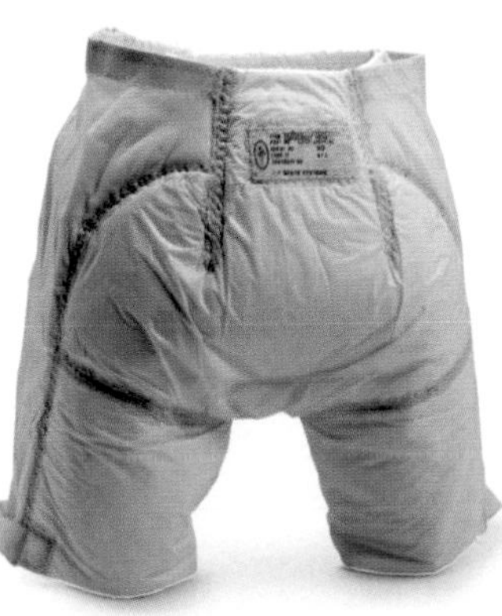

Space underwear
Extra-Vehicular Activities (EVAs) can last for several hours, so astronauts wear a "space diaper" for when they have to go to the bathroom.

Future technologies

In the future, astronauts may step onto Mars. More advanced, more flexible, and lighter spacesuits, such as this Z-series test spacesuit, are being designed for this moment. The Z-series spacesuit is designed to be easily adjustable to fit different body shapes.

BIG MOMENT

Suitsat
In 2006, ISS astronauts released into space an empty Orlan suit to see whether old spacesuits could be used as satellites or would overheat. "Suitsat" had a radio that transmitted signals for about two weeks before its batteries died.

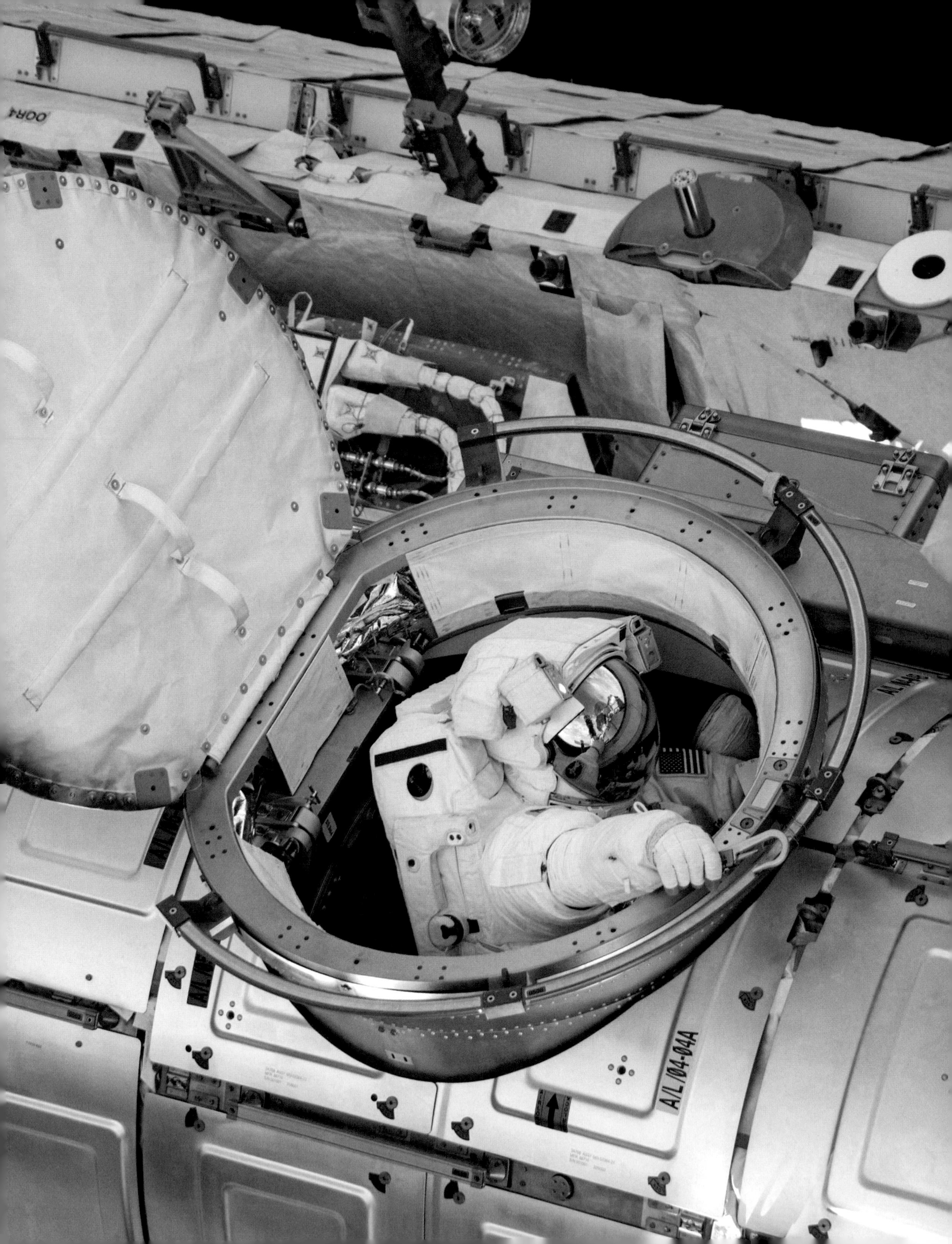
A/L/04-04A

DOOR TO SPACE

Astronauts say that the moment they emerge into space during an Extra-Vehicular Activity (EVA) is an unforgettable experience. Though they've already spent hours preparing themselves by going through a variety of safety procedures, the sight of Earth below and the inky vastness of space above takes their breath away—at least until it's time for work.

Tight squeeze

Before venturing outside, astronauts allow their bodies to adjust to breathing their suit's pure oxygen air supply. Here, US astronauts Michael Foale and Bernard A. Harris Jr. wait in the cramped airlock of the space shuttle *Discovery*. Harris became the first Black American astronaut to walk in space during a Shuttle-Mir mission in 1995.

DID YOU KNOW?

Doing light exercise helps astronauts adjust more quickly to the pure oxygen atmosphere inside their spacesuits.

◀ Emerging from the airlock

Once most of the air has been pumped out of the airlock, the last traces are vented into space. Final checks confirm there are no suit leaks, and the astronauts double- and triple-check that their tethers are attached before they open the hatch and float out. A circular rail around the hatch allows them to hold on and reattach their tethers to the station's exterior.

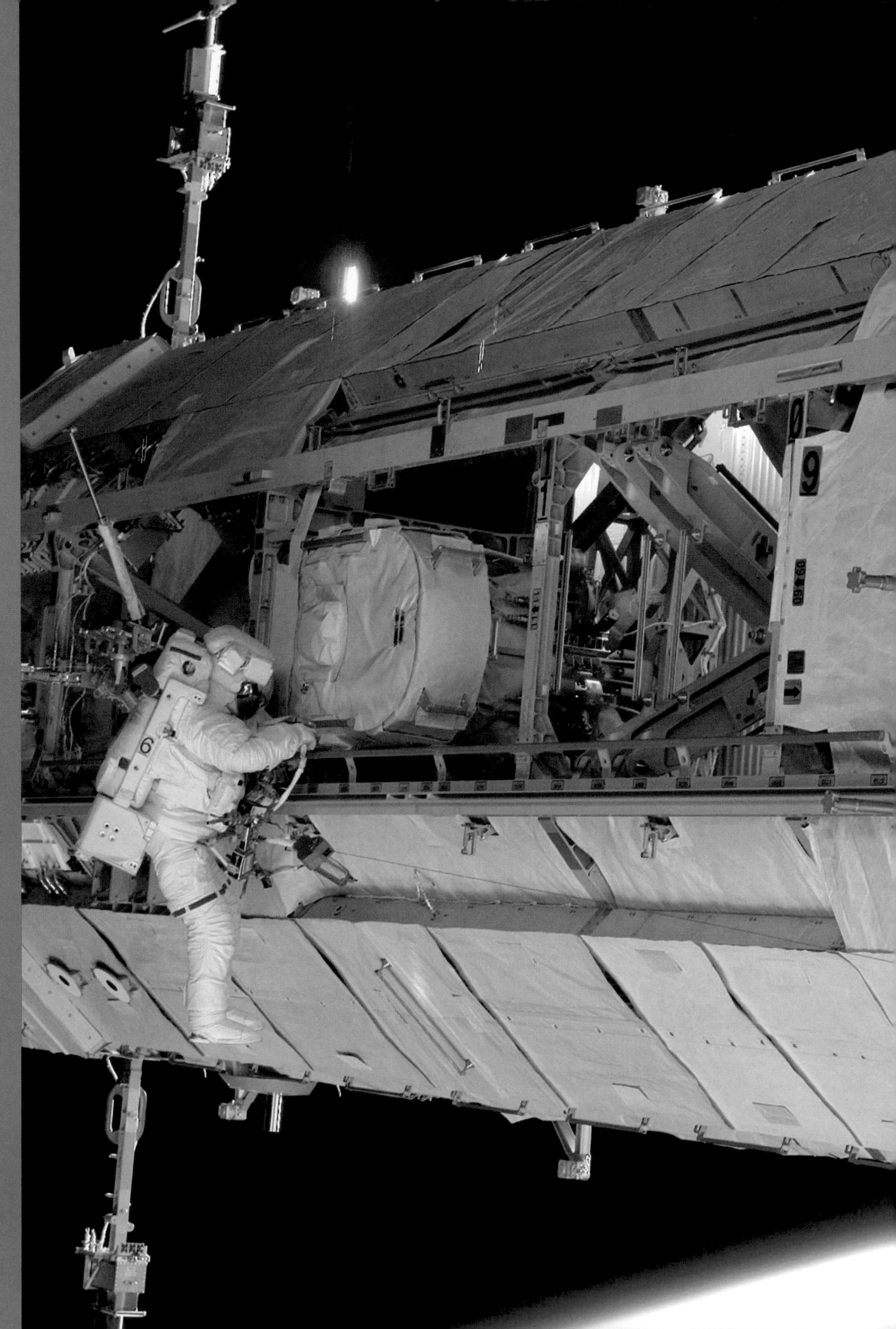

A WALK OUTDOORS

Spacewalks, officially known as Extra-Vehicular Activities (EVAs), are a tiring but exciting highlight of any space mission. Astronauts float out of the ISS to install new parts, carry out routine maintenance, and make repairs. They go out in pairs, and each EVA is carefully planned months in advance to make sure everyone knows what they're doing.

◄ Building the ISS

Astronauts performed more than 150 EVAs between 1998 and 2011 to construct the ISS. US astronauts Richard Mastracchio and Clayton Anderson, pictured here, can be seen placing equipment on the station's truss (central spine) during a spacewalk in 2007. Driverless "carts" that slide back and forth along the truss carry astronauts and their gear, saving them the trouble of "walking" across the length of the station.

Safety handrails
Mounted on the exterior of the ISS are handrails for astronauts to grip and remain stable while they work. Astronauts can grasp these handrails to move themselves easily around the station. They can also attach their ropes (tethers) to them to ensure they don't drift off into space.

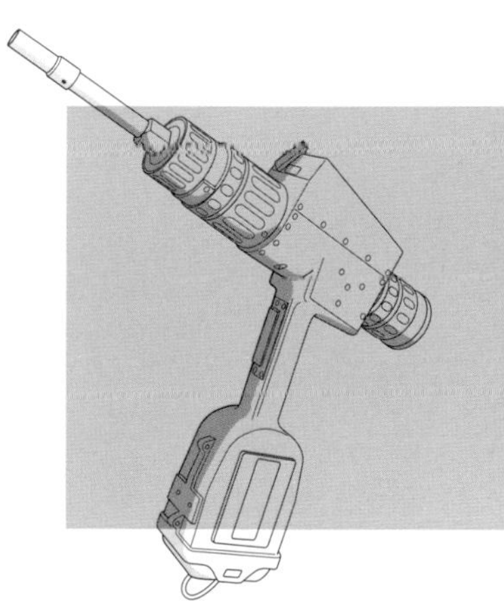

BIG MOMENT

First woman spacewalker
In July 1984, Russian cosmonaut Svetlana Savitskaya became the first woman to walk in space. She floated out of the Salyut 7 space station to conduct a series of experiments during a spacewalk that lasted more than three hours.

SPACEWALK GADGETS

From cameras to power tools, spacewalking astronauts must remember some essential items when they head outside the station. They often take photographs for scientists and engineers back on Earth, who then review the pictures to check on equipment. During a 2018 spacewalk, US astronaut Mark Vande Hei clicked a self-portrait, popularly known as a "space selfie," by using a camera and his shiny helmet visor as a mirror.

Camera kit
A camera used during a spacewalk must be padded with insulation to protect it against extreme temperatures. It can be attached to the user's spacesuit.

Power tools

Some tools, like this "pistol-grip" power drill, are designed to be operated while wearing thick gloves, so they're easier to use on a spacewalk.

Lost in space
In 2008, a toolbag slipped out of an astronaut's hand during an EVA. It later burned up in Earth's atmosphere.

SUPER SPACE-WALKS

Sometimes, astronauts have to “walk” in space to carry out repairs to the space station from the outside, test new tools, or perform experiments. The first few spacewalks (EVAs) lasted only a few minutes, but now they may go on for as long as eight hours. Spacewalks are physically challenging and not without risk. Despite lots of preparation, they don’t always go quite as planned.

FIRST SPACEWALK

Russian cosmonaut Alexei Leonov went on the very first spacewalk during the *Voskhod* 2 mission in March 1965. Problems with the air pressure inside his spacesuit caused it to expand so much that he had to let out some air to safely reenter the spacecraft.

First US spacewalk
In June 1965, US astronaut Ed White became the first American to walk in space.

LIFE JACKET

In September 1994, US astronauts used a new “life jacket” for spacewalks. Called SAFER (Simplified Aid For EVA Rescue), it is a jet pack that allows astronauts to return to the space station if they become separated from it.

CHINA’S FIRST SPACEWALK

Chinese taikonaut Zhai Zhigang went on a 20-minute walk outside the *Shenzhou* 7 spacecraft in September 2008. He was the first person from his country to walk successfully in space. His achievement was broadcast live on Chinese television.

Pick-up service
Zhigang collects experiment samples from the exterior of his spacecraft.

FLOATING FREE

In February 1984, US astronaut Bruce McCandless went on an EVA without tying himself to his spacecraft with a tether (rope). He used a backpack called the Manned Maneuvering Unit (MMU), which released small bursts of nitrogen gas to move him.

320 feet

The distance McCandless traveled away from the spacecraft.

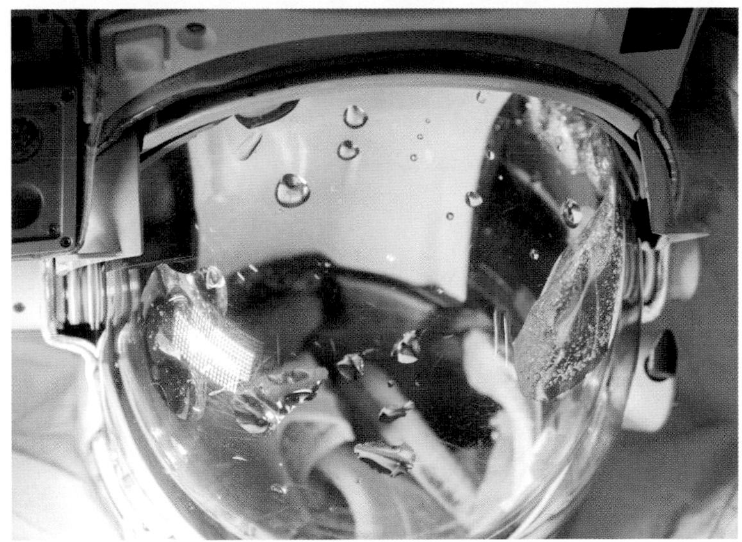

UNEXPECTED PROBLEMS

In July 2013, Italian astronaut Luca Parmitano had to make an emergency return to the ISS after a problem in his spacesuit's cooling system caused his helmet to begin to fill up with water while he was out on a spacewalk.

ALL-FEMALE SPACEWALK

In October 2019, US astronauts Christina Koch and Jessica Meir made history by going on the first all-female EVA—a spacewalk to replace a power unit on the ISS. The EVA was originally planned for March 2019, but it had to be postponed because there was only one medium-sized spacesuit on board.

5.5 hours

The duration of the first all-female spacewalk.

BEST OF THE REST

▶ FIRST EVA BY A NON-RUSSIAN, NON-AMERICAN

In December 1988, French astronaut Jean-Loup Chrétien became the first non-Russian, non-American person to perform a spacewalk.

▶ FIRST THREE-PERSON EVA

In 1992, US astronauts Thomas Akers, Richard Hieb, and Pierre Thuot made the first three-person EVA. They were aboard the space shuttle *Endeavour*.

▶ LONGEST TIME SPENT SPACEWALKING

Russian cosmonaut Anatoly Solovyev flew into space five times and spent a total of 82 hours and 22 minutes on spacewalks.

HEADING HOME

The end of an ISS mission is a busy time, with some of the station crew getting ready to head home, while the rest stay onboard to join the next mission. There are photos to be taken, souvenirs to collect, ceremonies and traditions to go through, and goodbyes to be said. Before departure, astronauts have to carry out checks on all their equipment—including making sure that they can still squeeze into their spacesuits after getting taller during months of weightlessness.

Signing off

American ISS Commander Sunita Williams adds her Expedition 33 mission patch to a row of others stuck to the station's walls by earlier astronauts. Shortly before returning home, the commander leaving the station hands over control to a new commander.

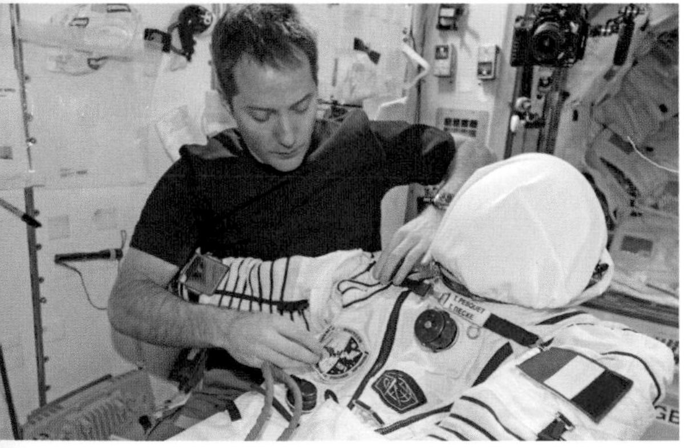

Moving on

The crew last wore their Sokol suits during the launch, which was technically a different expedition, and so the mission patches on their suits have become out of date. Before returning home, the crew must update the mission patch to represent the current mission.

▶ Tight squeeze

Astronauts prepare for their return by rehearsing the undocking, reentry, and landing procedures. The Soyuz descent module is even more cramped on the return journey because astronauts get about 2 in (5 cm) taller in space and may no longer fit comfortably into their seats.

DID YOU KNOW?

It takes about three hours to return to Earth from the space station.

BACK TO EARTH

While many early space station crews enjoyed a fairly smooth glide back to Earth aboard the space shuttle, between 2011 and 2020, the only way to come home was in a small, bell-shaped reentry crew capsule of the Russian Soyuz called the descent module. It was a safe but fiery descent through Earth's atmosphere—a ride that can be extremely bumpy for the passengers!

▶ Welcome party

Astronauts usually wait in their capsule until someone comes to help them out, as their muscles are weakened after months in space. But as the landing zone is in a remote area of Kazakhstan, the crew are trained to survive in the wilderness if they come down too far away from their target.

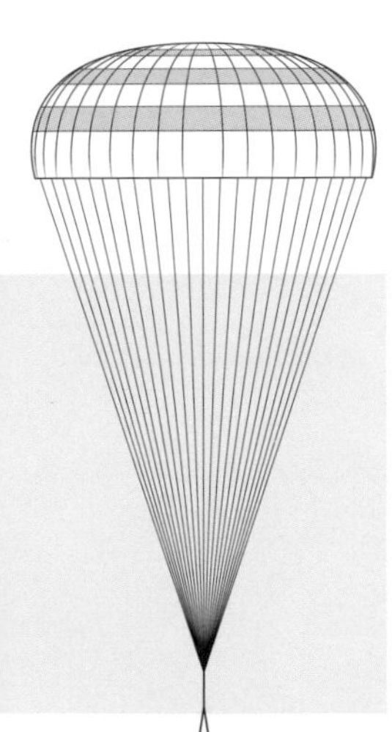

Recovery vehicle

Using scientific calculations and simulations, it's possible to predict when and where a spacecraft will land. A huge ground operation team swings into action with helicopters and all-terrain vehicles, like this one below, on standby for the landing.

The journey home

Just as a spacecraft needs to reach incredibly high speeds to travel into space, it must do the opposite and slow down to come back to Earth and make a safe landing. The Soyuz does this in several dramatic stages. With no wheels or wings, it doesn't land like an airplane—instead, it slows down with the help of a parachute.

1 After undocking from the station, the Soyuz turns so it is flying "backward," and its rockets fire to slow it down. Two of its modules are discarded since they are no longer needed.

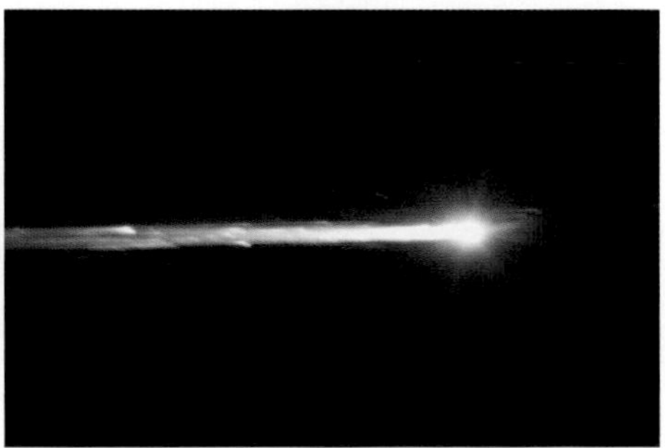

2 Traveling at 17,000 mph (27,000 kph), the descent module reenters Earth's atmosphere. Compression of the air in front of the speeding spacecraft causes it to heat up. The crew loses contact with mission control for about six minutes.

After reentry, the module slows to 500 mph (800 kph). A small parachute opens to reduce its speed more, then the main parachute opens to lower it to the ground.

The module, which can be used only once, nears the ground at 25 ft per second (7.8 m per second). Rockets on its base fire just above the ground to slow it further, then it touches down.

Splashdown landing

In contrast to the Soyuz, the SpaceX Dragon spacecraft splashes down at sea, using water rather than rockets to cushion its landing. It floats until recovery ships arrive.

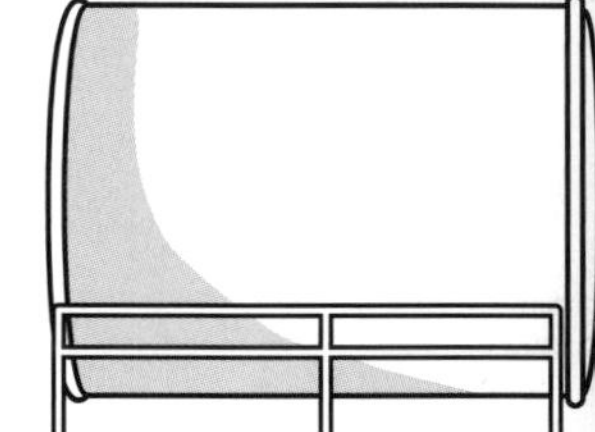

FUTURE MISSIONS

There have been astronauts living on the ISS for more than 20 years. During that time, scientists and engineers have learned so much about life in microgravity. Now, they are looking to the future. What will it take to put more people into space? How could we one day make it back to the Moon or even to Mars? Long-duration missions have shown us what day-to-day challenges might face the first travelers to the Red Planet. Back on Earth, simulations are revealing how humans might physically and mentally handle long-term confinement and isolation. Using this hard-earned knowledge, space agencies and private companies are planning new, exciting missions that reach farther into our Solar System than ever before.

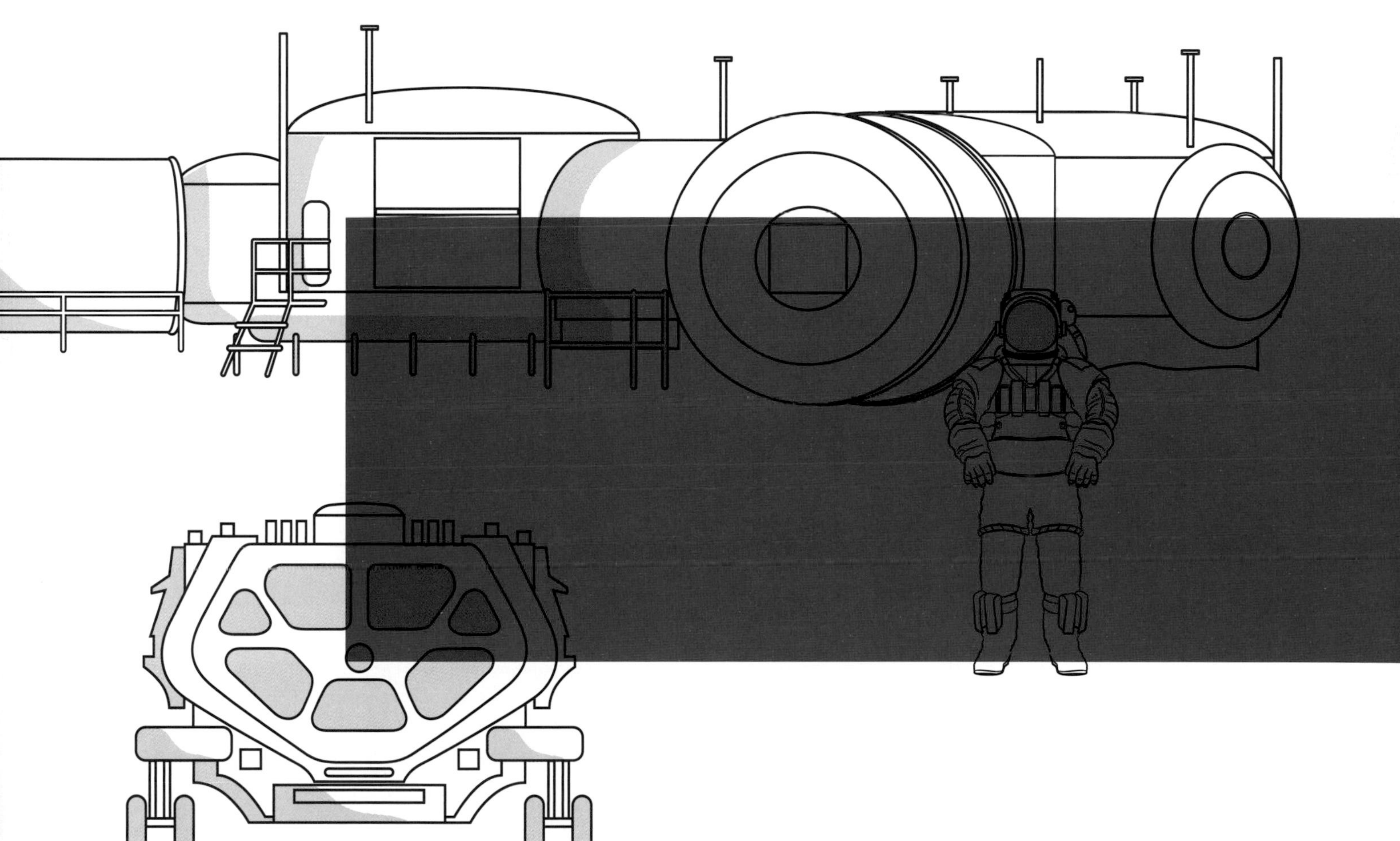

DID YOU KNOW?

During the MARS-500 experiment in 2010–11, six volunteers stayed in isolation for 520 days—the length of a possible mission to Mars.

ANALOG MISSIONS

Since space travel is so expensive, one of the best ways to prepare for future missions is to find—or create—conditions on Earth that are similar to the extreme environments experienced in space. Space agencies recruit volunteers, including astronauts, to test how well they handle living in cramped spaces or spending long periods in isolation. These so-called analog missions are also used to simulate the conditions encountered on other planets.

◀ NASA Desert RATS

NASA's Desert Research And Training Studies program (Desert RATS) conducted trials in the arid deserts of Arizona to test new equipment and technologies that could be used for exploring the Moon, asteroids, and even Mars. These included spacesuits, robots, rovers, and new communication systems.

Isolation research

NASA's Human Exploration Research Analog (HERA) is an isolated habitat in which volunteers take part in simulated space missions of up to 45 days. They endure some of the challenges of space, such as living in a confined space and experiencing communication delays.

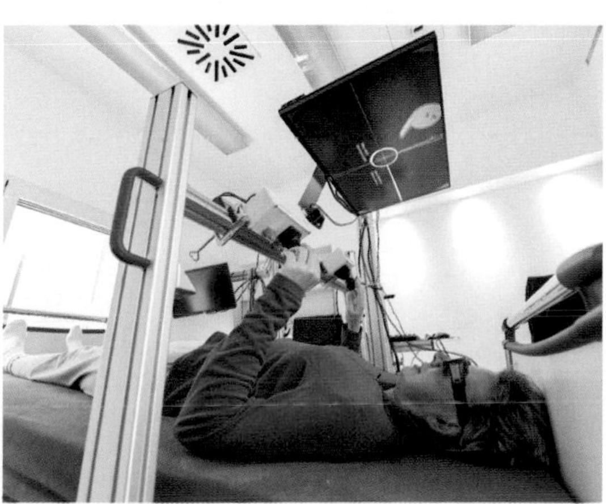

Bed rest research

During bed rest studies, volunteers are monitored while they spend up to 10 weeks lying in beds that tilt slightly downward toward their heads. The effects on the body are similar to those experienced in microgravity, allowing doctors to research ways of keeping future astronauts healthy.

UNDERWATER LABORATORY

On Earth, living and working at the bottom of the sea is perhaps the closest you can get to the isolation and confinement of a space mission. NASA's Extreme Environment Mission Operations (NEEMO) project sends astronauts, scientists, and engineers on missions up to three weeks long to Aquarius, an underwater lab off the coast of Florida, 62 ft (19 m) below the ocean surface.

Practice run

Being inside Aquarius is similar to being on the space station. The crew, nicknamed "aquanauts," live and work in a small space, separated from people on the surface and with challenging conditions outside.

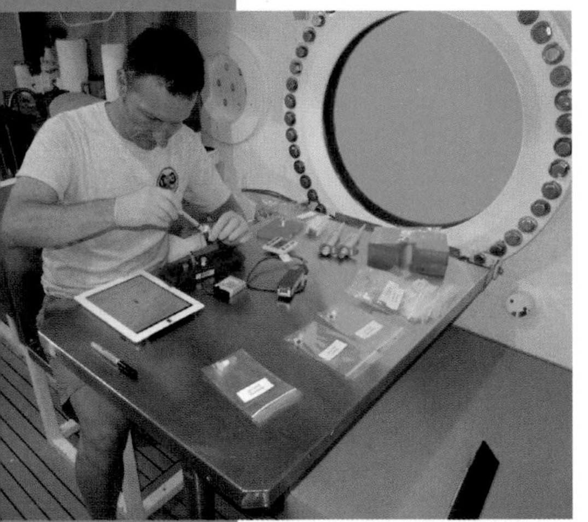

Sea scientists
German astronaut Matthias Maurer is pictured here doing an experiment during a 2016 practice mission to Mars. Conditions were made to be as realistic as possible. Messages from Mars can take about 17 minutes to reach Earth, so mission control delayed incoming and outgoing communications.

Prepared for anything
During her 2015 mission on Aquarius, US astronaut Serena Auñón-Chancellor headed out onto the seafloor in scuba gear to test equipment that may one day be used for spacewalks on the Moon, Mars, or even asteroids.

DID YOU KNOW?

The name NEEMO refers to Captain Nemo, the famous submariner in French author Jules Verne's novel *20,000 Leagues Under the Sea*.

NASA
NASA

DREAM HOLIDAY

You don't necessarily have to be a professional astronaut to travel to space, although you do need lots of money. Between 2000 and 2009, the ISS welcomed several paying guests for visits lasting 8–12 days. More recently, a number of private companies have launched their own crewed flights, with spaces available for paying travelers to take brief but thrilling trips to the edge of space.

▶ Ahead of the game

In the 2000s, seven space tourists, also known as spaceflight participants, traveled to the ISS as paying passengers on Russian Soyuz missions. The first was US engineer Dennis Tito, who paid $20 million for his eight-day trip to orbit in 2001. The last of these early tourist flights took place in 2009. The retirement of the space shuttle in 2011 meant that seats on Soyuz flights to the ISS were needed for astronauts.

Private travel into space

In 2021, two private companies—Virgin Galactic and Blue Origin—launched their first successful crewed flights. Both run short suborbital trips to the edge of space, about 62 miles (100 km) above Earth's surface.

Blue Origin
Blue Origin's pilotless space capsule is launched by a reusable rocket to an altitude of around 66 miles (107 km) before it parachutes back to Earth.

Virgin Galactic
The VSS *Unity* spacecraft flies to a high altitude beneath a carrier plane before rocketing to the edge of space. It glides for a few minutes and then returns to the ground.

DID YOU KNOW?

Iranian-born engineer and entrepreneur Anousheh Ansari visited the ISS in 2006, becoming the first female space tourist.

dearMoon project

Japanese billionaire Yusaku Maezawa's 2023 dearMoon project is perhaps the most ambitious space tourism trip ever imagined. Maezawa plans to take eight civilian guests on a figure-eight loop around Earth and the Moon aboard SpaceX's new Starship spacecraft.

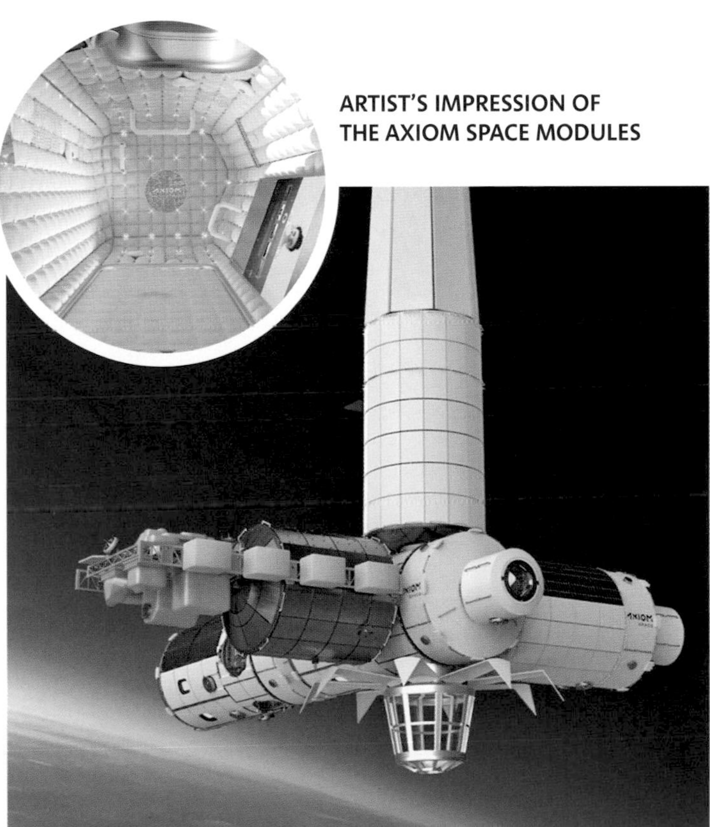

ARTIST'S IMPRESSION OF THE AXIOM SPACE MODULES

Future station

To accommodate tourists and other commercial activities in space, NASA has joined forces with a private company, Axiom Space, to create comfortable, beautifully designed habitable modules by the mid-2020s. The modules will initially be attached to the ISS, but later they'll be separated to form an independent space station operated by Axiom Space.

NEW MISSION

The September 2021 launch of Inspiration4—the first all-civilian space mission—represented the start of a new era that could see space travel become increasingly possible for ordinary people and not just professional astronauts. Operated by the private spaceflight company SpaceX and paid for by US entrepreneur Jared Isaacman, Inspiration4's spacecraft *Resilience*—which also delivers supplies to the ISS—spent three days orbiting Earth at an altitude of 360 miles (575 km)—that's more than 100 miles (150 km) higher than the ISS.

▼ Trailblazers in space

The Inspiration4 crew were chosen because they represented the spaceflight's four "mission pillars." Pictured from left to right, hospital donor Chris Sembroski stood for generosity and cancer survivor Hayley Arceneaux was selected as a symbol of hope. As commander, Isaacman himself symbolized leadership, and scientist and entrepreneur Dr. Sian Proctor represented prosperity.

Mission inspiration

The mission raised more than $200 million for research into childhood cancers at St. Jude's Children's Research Hospital in Tennessee. Crew member Arceneaux was once a patient at St. Jude's and later joined the hospital as a physician's assistant. She is the first person with a prosthetic (artificial) limb to fly in space.

***RESILIENCE* CAPSULE**

Splashdown

After 71 hours in orbit, during which the crew enjoyed the view, took part in experiments, listened to music, and made art, the *Resilience* capsule splashed into the sea off Florida, within sight of recovery boats.

DID YOU KNOW?

Dr. Sian Proctor was the first Black woman to be assigned to pilot a spacecraft.

Enjoying the view
As *Resilience* wasn't docking with the ISS, its docking port was replaced with a huge domed window. With a diameter of 46 in (1.16 m), it provided the crew with spectacular 360° views.

▲ Gateway to the Moon

A space station orbiting the Moon forms a key part of NASA's Artemis Program, which aims to land humans on the lunar surface for the first time since 1972. Planned for launch in 2024, the Lunar Gateway station (shown in this illustration) will have just two modules at first but can grow over time.

Base camp on the Moon
This illustration shows Artemis Base Camp, where astronauts can live for up to two months at a time. When at its closest to the Moon, the Lunar Gateway will be used to drop off and meet landers traveling to and from the new base. At the farthest points on its orbit, it will study the Moon from above.

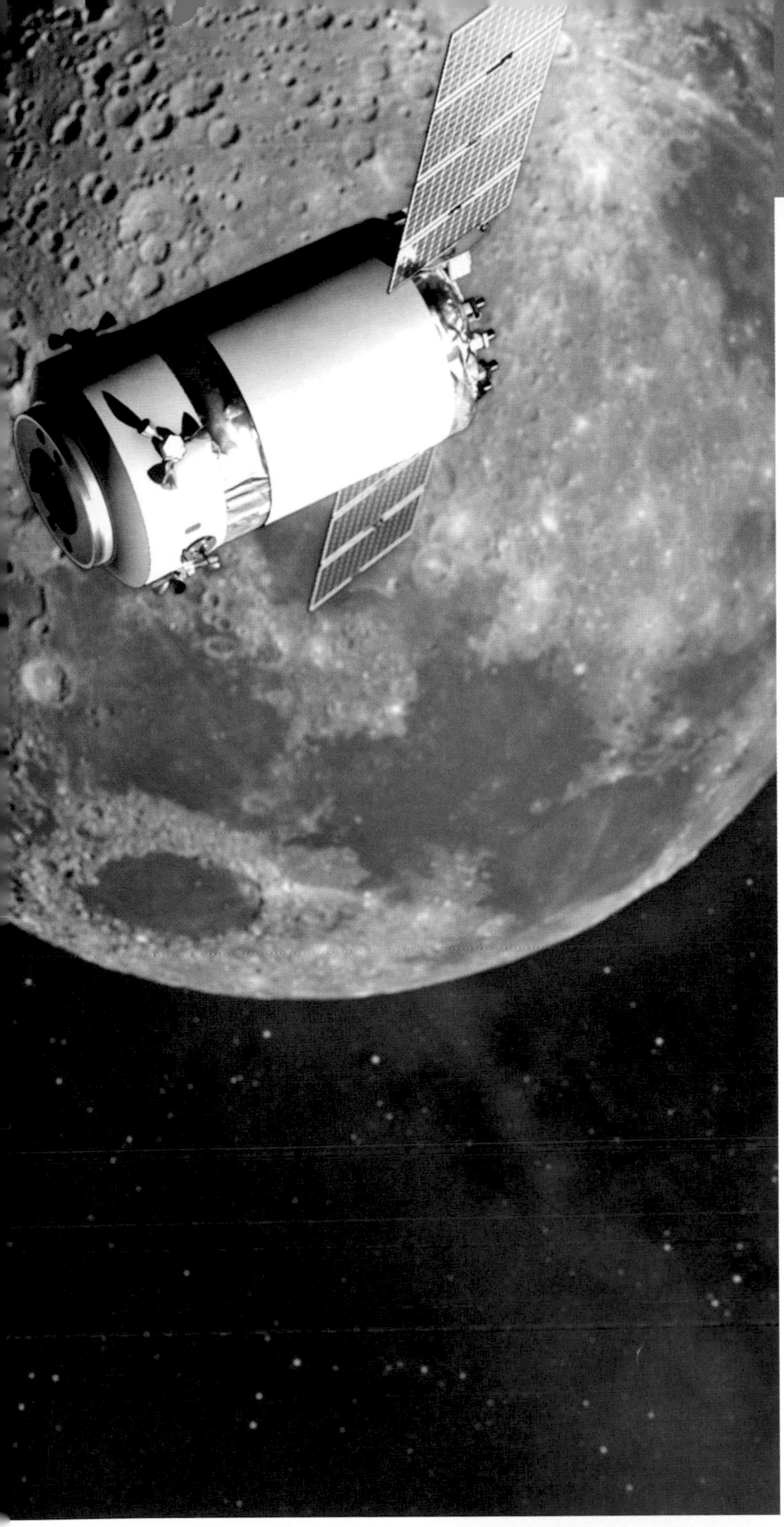

THE FUTURE OF SPACE STATIONS

The ISS can't last forever. Even with regular maintenance and new modules added, critical parts will gradually wear out. All nations involved have agreed to pay for the station until at least 2024, and it is built to last until 2028 and beyond, but one day its mission will end. So what happens then?

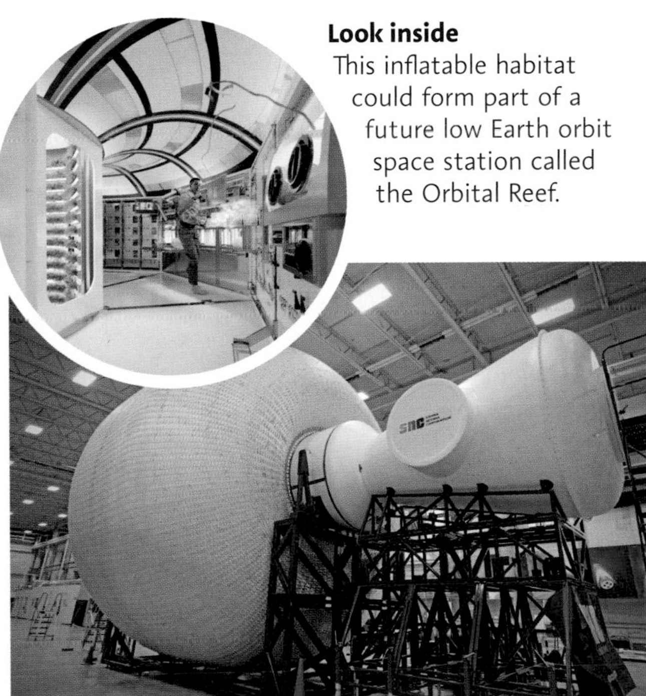

Look inside
This inflatable habitat could form part of a future low Earth orbit space station called the Orbital Reef.

Credit: Sierra Space Corporation

What follows the ISS?

Private companies are already developing space station plans. US company Axiom Space is designing a module, due to be attached to the ISS, which will later become the core of another independent station. US companies Blue Origin and Sierra Space are also planning to build a low Earth orbit space station called the Orbital Reef.

Made in space

Future space stations—as well as missions to the Moon and Mars—may make their own spare parts and tools in orbit. 3D printing technology has been tested on the ISS since 2014 and could be used to create items based on designs sent from Earth.

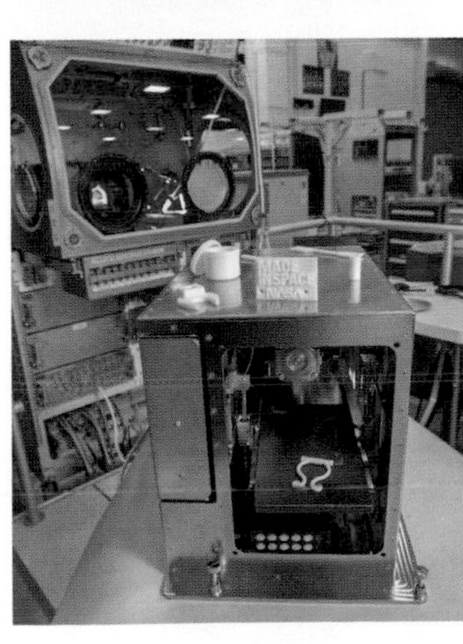

WHAT IS NEXT?

Research carried out on the ISS provides scientists and engineers with plenty of knowledge to develop space missions that reach farther into the Solar System. Journeys beyond the Moon to Mars or nearby asteroids will take many months or years and will require complex spacecraft. In years to come, when humanity sets off on such missions, space stations may play a vital role as essential stopping points along the way.

▶ Mars outpost

Some plans to establish a base on Mars call for a space station to be built in the planet's orbit before a human landing takes place. However it happens, the first astronauts on Mars will draw on the docking techniques, technologies for processing air and water, and even the space gardening skills pioneered aboard the ISS.

Is there life on other planets?

ISS experiments have shown that living things can exist in the hostile conditions of space. But could there actually be life beyond Earth? Rovers on the Red Planet have found no signs of life so far, and radio telescopes on Earth haven't yet detected any signals from intelligent aliens, but there is still much we don't know about our Solar System and beyond.

DID YOU KNOW?

Mars rover *Perseverance* carried out an experiment that converted carbon dioxide in the planet's atmosphere into breathable oxygen.

PLACES TO VISIT

A visit to a space station might not be possible for everyone. But back on Earth, there are plenty of museums and other places where you can get up close to retired spacecraft, historic spacesuits, and other amazing objects linked to the history of spaceflight. Some space agencies, such as NASA and ESA, even have tours that allow visitors to get an exclusive, behind-the-scenes look at some of their facilities.

SMITHSONIAN NATIONAL AIR AND SPACE MUSEUM

With two sites, one in Washington, D.C., and the other in Virginia, the Smithsonian National Air and Space Museum has a huge range of iconic objects to see, including the space shuttle *Discovery*. Visitors can also experience a virtual reality spacewalk.

NATIONAL SPACE CENTER, UK

A visit to the National Space Center in Leicester, UK, begins with the enormous Rocket Tower at the entrance. There are spacesuits, satellites, and meteorites on display and a show to see in the center's domed planetarium.

The Rocket Tower
Inside the center's enormous Rocket Tower is a 88.5 ft (27 m) tall US rocket called Thor Able.

CHINA AEROSPACE MUSEUM, CHINA

Located in Beijing, China, this museum celebrates the country's rapidly expanding space program. There are rockets, spacesuits, satellites, and spacecraft to see as well as exhibits devoted to China's past and current Tiangong space stations. It's being refurbished and reopens in 2023.

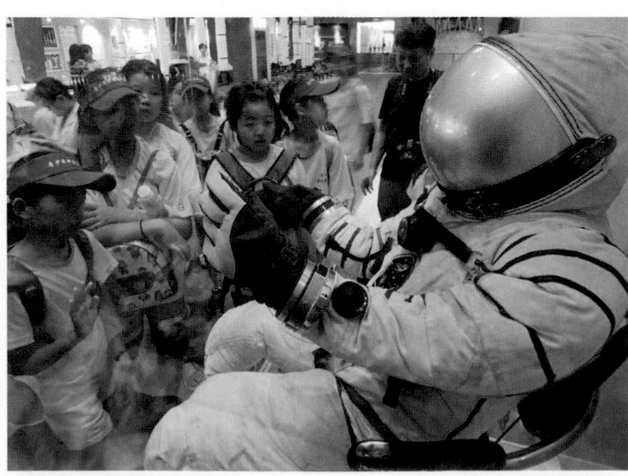

STAR CITY, RUSSIA

The history of the Gagarin Cosmonaut Training Center in Star City, Russia, goes all the way back to the 1950s and the start of the Space Age. Huge water tanks, once used by cosmonauts to train for spacewalks, are on display. You can try wearing a spacesuit and even taste space food.

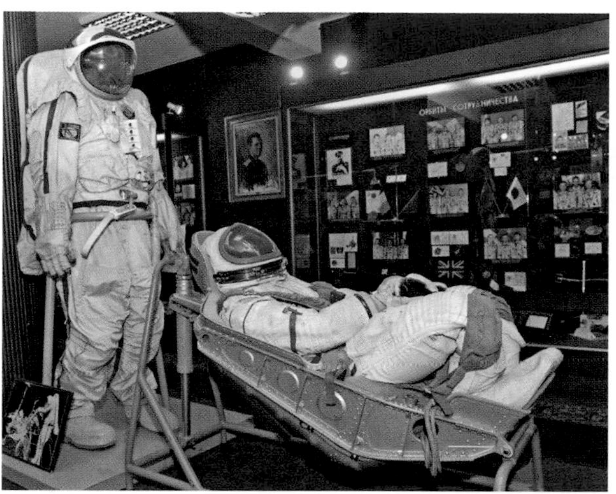

ESOC, GERMANY

During public and private tours of the European Space Operations Center (ESOC) in Darmstadt, Germany, visitors get to see firsthand what happens behind the scenes in some of the mission control rooms dedicated to various ESA missions.

Get up close
Visitors take a close look at a model of a satellite on display outside ESOC.

TSUKUBA SPACE CENTER, JAPAN

This space center features a life-size, exact replica of *Kibo*, a Japanese science module on the ISS. You'll also discover a huge model of Japan's Kounotori spacecraft—used for resupplying the space station—as well as a beautiful scale model of Earth.

1972

The year the Tsukuba Space Center opened.

WHERE TO GO NEXT

▶ AUSTRALIAN SPACE DISCOVERY CENTER, AUSTRALIA

This space center opened in Adelaide in 2021. Here, the latest space technology is on display, and visitors can learn all about Australia's growing space industry.

▶ JEJU AEROSPACE MUSEUM, SOUTH KOREA

This museum on Jeju Island focuses on the history of aviation, space, and astronomy.

▶ KENNEDY SPACE CENTER

NASA's main launch facility in Florida offers tours. Its many exhibits include tools from historic flights and a "rocket garden" featuring different types of rockets.

GLOSSARY

Airlock
A small sealed room that stops air in a spacecraft from escaping into space; astronauts enter or exit the spacecraft through this room

Air pressure
The force of air pushing against objects; also called atmospheric pressure

Altitude
The height of an object, spacecraft, or place above sea or ground level

Analog mission
Simulations carried out on Earth that replicate certain space mission conditions, such as confinement and isolation; they help scientists research the effects of long-duration space travel

Asteroid
A small, rocky object that orbits the Sun

Astronaut
A person trained to travel to space and live and work there

Atmosphere
The layer of gas that surrounds a planet

Aurora
A display of glowing gas in a planet's upper atmosphere, most often over its polar regions

CAPCOM
Capsule Communicator—a person working in mission control who communicates with astronauts in space

Capsule
A small spacecraft or part of a larger one; it usually carries crew or equipment

Cargo
Equipment carried on a spacecraft

Cell
The smallest building block of all living beings; humans are made up of millions of cells

CNSA
China National Space Administration—the Chinese national space agency

Commander
The lead astronaut of a mission

Cosmic radiation
High-energy particles released by the Sun, stars, and other phenomena that can be harmful for astronauts

Cosmonaut
A Russian astronaut

Crew
The group of astronauts who work and live on a spacecraft

Cupola
An ISS observatory module with seven windows, built by the European Space Agency

Docking
When a spacecraft, like the Soyuz, attaches to another spacecraft, such as the ISS, in space

Eclipse
When an object either passes into the shadow of another object or temporarily blocks an observer's view; during a solar eclipse, the Moon moves between the Sun and Earth, causing a shadow to fall on Earth

Engineer
A person who designs or builds technical equipment; often they are trained in math

ESA
European Space Agency; members include 22 European countries with a space program

EVA
Extra-Vehicular Activity; see also *Spacewalk*

Flight controller
A person who works in mission control; they guide astronauts as they carry out tasks in space and monitor and control systems on the ISS

Gravity
A force that attracts objects toward each other; on Earth, gravity attracts objects to the ground and gives them weight, and in space, it keeps the Moon and the ISS in Earth's orbit and Earth in the Sun's orbit

International Space Station (ISS)
The largest human-made structure in Earth's orbit. It functions as a unique scientific laboratory and home for astronauts in space

JAXA
Japan Aerospace Exploration Agency—the Japanese national space agency

Laboratory
A place where science experiments are performed

Launch
The process of using rockets to send something into space

Launchpad
The place, usually a platform with a support structure, from where a rocket launches into space

Low Earth orbit
An orbit between 100 miles (160 km) and 620 miles (1,000 km) above Earth's surface

Microgravity
A condition in which the force of gravity is present, but its effect is small; objects appear weightless in a microgravity (free fall) environment, like on the ISS

Mission
An uncrewed or crewed trip to space to carry out an activity

Mission control
On Earth, a team of flight controllers, engineers, and support staff, led by a flight director, who monitor missions from launch through to landing

Module
A part of a space station that can be used by crews and connected to another component

NASA
National Aeronautics and Space Administration—the US national space agency

Observatory
Any building that houses devices to look into space from Earth; there are also observatories in space that have equipment to view Earth, other planets, galaxies, and other objects in space

Orbit
The path an object takes around another object when attracted by its gravity—for example, Earth's orbit around the Sun

Payload
Cargo or equipment carried into space by a rocket or spacecraft

Penumbra
The light, outer part of a shadow cast by an object

Radiation
A form of energy, such as light and heat, found throughout the universe

Robot
A computer-controlled machine that can move and carry out tasks; some robots can sense their environment and have some ability to respond to it automatically

Rocket
A vehicle designed to carry spacecraft, satellites, and astronauts into space

Roscosmos
Roscosmos State Corporation for Space Activities—the Russian national space agency

Rover
A vehicle driven remotely across the surface of another planet, like Mars, or the Moon

Satellite
A natural or human-made object that moves around a larger object in space—for example, the Moon is Earth's natural satellite, and the ISS is a human-made satellite

Shenzhou
Chinese spacecraft designed to send taikonauts and cargo into space

Simulation
An event or situation designed to mimic the extreme environment of space on Earth; it is used to train astronauts for the challenges of living and working in space

Sokol suit
The emergency pressurized spacesuit worn by astronauts inside the Soyuz spacecraft; it can't be worn during an EVA

Solar
Related to the Sun

Soyuz
A Russian spacecraft used to carry cosmonauts and cargo between Earth and the ISS

Space
The place beyond Earth's atmosphere; also the name for the area between space bodies, such as planets, stars, and galaxies

Space agency
A national organization that manages activities relating to space exploration

Spacecraft
A vehicle designed to travel in space

Space debris
Orbiting pieces of space junk, which can include used rocket stages, old satellites, fragmentation debris, and even flecks of paint

Space Shuttle
A partially reusable spacecraft designed to transport astronauts and cargo into Earth's orbit

Space station
A space habitat that stays in Earth's orbit for a long period of time—for example, the ISS; astronauts can live and work there

Spacesuit
A specially designed sealed suit worn by astronauts to protect themselves during a spacewalk

Spacewalk
When an astronaut heads outside of a spacecraft into space, usually to test equipment or conduct repairs; also called Extra-Vehicular Activity (EVA)

Stage
The separate parts that make up a rocket; each part has its own engine and fuel tank

Taikonaut
A Chinese astronaut

Tether
A safety cord that attaches an astronaut to a spacecraft during an EVA

Thrust
The propulsive force of a rocket or other reaction engine

Tiangong
China's space station, currently being built in low Earth orbit

Ultraviolet (UV) rays
Short radiation waves produced by the Sun that are invisible to the human eye; UV rays are harmful for humans

Umbra
The dark, central part of a shadow cast by an object

Vacuum
An empty area with nothing in it—not even air

Virtual reality (VR)
A computer-generated world experienced through a headset

INDEX

Page numbers in **bold** refer to main entries.

ACKNOWLEDGMENTS

DK would like to thank the following people for their contribution:
Arshti Narang and Vaibhav Rastogi for additional design assistance; Suhita Dharamjit for design assistance on the jacket; Zaina Budaly and Ben Morgan for additional editorial assistance; Helen Peters for the index; and Jane Parker for proofreading.

Smithsonian Enterprises:
Kealy Gordon, Product Development Manager; Jill Corcoran, Director, Licensed Publishing; Brigid Ferraro, Vice President, Business Development and Licensing; Carol LeBlanc, President.

Smithsonian Curators:
National Air and Space Museum:
Dr. Jennifer Levasseur, Museum Curator, Department of Space History.

DK would like to thank the following for their kind permission to reproduce their photographs:
(Key: a-above; b-below/bottom; c-center; f-far; l-left; r-right; t-top)

10 NASA. 11 Alamy Stock Photo: John Gilbey (fbr); Stocktrek Images, Inc. (br). **ESA:** NASA (tr). **NASA:** Johnson Space Center (bl). **12 NASA:** (tl); Marshall Space Flight Center (bl). **12–13 NASA. 13 Alamy Stock Photo:** NC Collections (bc). **14–15 NASA:** ARC / Rick Guidice. **14 NASA:** Don Davis (bl). **16 Dorling Kindersley:** Gary Ombler / Dave Shayler / Astro Info Service Ltd (crb). **Getty Images:** Sovfoto / Universal Images Group (tr, cra). **NASA:** (br). **TopFoto:** Sputnik (bl). **17 Dorling Kindersley:** Gary Ombler / Dave Shayler / Astro Info Service Ltd (tr). **Dreamstime.com:** Viocara (cr). **Getty Images:** Erik Simonsen (cb). **NASA:** (tl, clb). **SPACEBOOSTERS Limited:** NASA (crb). **20–21 ESA:** Roscosmo. **21 Canadian Space Agency (CSA):** (r/c). **ESA:** (r/d). **Japan Aerospace Exploration Agency (JAXA):** (r/e). **NASA:** (r/a). **State Space Corporation Roscosmos:** (r/b). **22–23 Roland Miller. 23 Roland Miller:** (tl, tr). **24–25 NASA:** Johnson Space Center. **25 Getty Images:** AFP / Bruce Weaver (bc). **NASA:** Johnson Space Center (cr); (br). **26–27 NASA. 26 NASA:** Johnson Space Center (cl); Armstrong Flight Research Center (bl). **Science Photo Library:** NASA (tl). **27 Alamy Stock Photo:** REUTERS (br). **NASA:** Kennedy Space Center (bl, cl). **28–29 NASA:** Johnson Space Center. **28 Alamy Stock Photo:** NG Images (cb). **29 ESA:** NASA (cl). **NASA:** Johnson Space Center (tl, tr, bl). **30–31 NASA. 30 ESA:** Alexander Gerst (bc). **NASA:** Johnson Space Center (cl). **31 NASA:** Johnson Space Center (br). **32–33 NASA. 32 NARA National Museum:** NASA / Johnson Space Center (crb). **33 NASA:** Kennedy Space Center / Frank Michaux (bc); Johnson Space Center (br). **34 NASA:** CANADIAN SPACE AGENCY (br, bc); ODPO (bl). **34–35 NASA. 35 ESA:** (br). **NASA:** (cb). **Texas A & M University:** (bl). **36 NASA:** Goddard / Chris Gunn (tl); Ben Smegelsky (crb). **36–37 NASA:** Ben Smegelsky. **37 NASA:** GRC / Bridget Caswell (tr); Isaac Watson (bl). **38 Getty Images:** Sergei Karpukhin\TASS (cl). **38–39 Getty Images:** Alexander Ryumin\TASS (b). **39 NASA:** (tl). **40–41 Reuters:** China Stringer Network (t). **40 Reuters:** Stringer Shanghai (bl). **Shutterstock.com:** Hap / Quirky China News (br). **41 Alamy Stock Photo:** REUTERS (br). **Reuters:** China Stringer Network (bl). **42 Dorling Kindersley: Dreamstime.com:** Alejandro Miranda (tl). **42–43 Getty Images:** China Manned Space :Engineering O / AFP (bl). **43 Alamy Stock Photo:** Xinhua (tl). **Getty Images:** Feature China / Barcroft Media (crb); Kevin Frayer (bl). **46–47 Getty Images:** NASA. **46 Getty Images:** Matt Stroshane (bl). **NASA:** KSC (cla, ca); Ben Smegelsky (bc). **47 Alamy Stock Photo:** UPI (cra). **Getty Images:** Epsilon (crb). **48–49 NASA. 48 NASA:** (br, fbr). **49 Alamy Stock Photo:** NASA Photo (bl). **NASA:** Joel Kowsky (br). **50 Alamy Stock Photo:** Bob Daemmrich (br). **NASA:** Carla Thomas (clb); Bill White (tr). **51 ESA:** S. Corvaja, 2014 (cla). **NASA:** Kim Shiflett (clb, tr). **52 Getty Images:** Stanislav Krasilnikov\TASS (cb). **52–53 ESA:** Stephane Corvaja. **53 ESA:** Stephane Corvaja (br). **54–55 Courtesy of U.S. Navy:** Robert Markowitz (tc). **54 Science Photo Library:** David Ducros (crb). **55 ESA:** Stephane Corvaja (br); Anneke Le Floc'h (tr, cr). **Getty Images:** Stanislav Krasilnikov\TASS (bc). **56–57 ESA:** Stephane Corvaja. **57 ESA:** Stephane Corvaja (tc); NASA / J. Blai (br). **58–59 NASA:** Johnson Space Center (r). **58 ESA:** Stephane Corvaja (cla). **NASA:** Johnson Space Center / Bill Stafford (clb). **60 ESA:** D. Baumbach, 2010 (tr); NASA / Vittorio Crobu (bl, cl). **NASA:** SpaceX (cr). **61 NASA:** Johnson Space Center / Robert Markowitz (tr); Johnson Space Center / Victor Zelentsov (cla). **62 NASA:** Bill Ingalls (bc); Joel Kowsky (tc). **Science & Society Picture Library:** (r). **63 Alamy Stock Photo:** NG Images (bc); SBS TV / Sipa Press (tc). **Japan Aerospace Exploration Agency (JAXA):** (tr, cr). **NASA:** GCTC / Andrey Shelepin. **64–65 NASA:** Johnson Space Center. **65 Alamy Stock Photo:** dpa picture alliance archive (bc). **Getty Images:** NASA / Bill Ingall (c). **Japan Aerospace Exploration Agency (JAXA):** (cb). **66 Getty Images:** Sergei Savostyanov\TASS (bl). **NASA:** Johnson Space Center / Andrey Shelepin / Gagarin Cosmonaut Training Cente (tr); Joel Kowsky (br). **67 Alamy Stock Photo:** NASA Image Collection (cra); Sergei Savostyanov / TASS (bl). **NASA:** Johnson Space Center / Victor Zelentso (tl); Bill Ingalls (tr). **68–69 NASA:** Bill Ingalls (c). **68 NASA:** Bill Ingalls (cl); Victor Zelentsov (tl). **69 NASA:** Bill Ingalls (tl, br). **70–71 NASA:** Johnson Space Center (t). **70 NASA:** Bill Ingalls (bl). **71 NASA:** Johnson Space Center (bc, cb). **72–73 NASA:** Bill Ingalls (b). **72 NASA:** Kennedy Space Center (bl). **SpaceX:** (tl). **73 Alamy Stock Photo:** SpaceX (br). **NASA:** Bill Ingalls (tc); Joel Kowsky (tr). **SpaceX:** (cra, cr). **74 Alamy Stock Photo:** Xinhua / Ma Yan (br). **NASA:** Johnson Space Center (tr); Kennedy Space Center (clb); Bill Ingalls (bc). **75 NASA:** Johnson Space Center (cla, crb); Carla Cioffi (tr). **76–77 NASA:** Johnson Space Center / Lauren Harnet. **76 NASA:** Johnson Space Center (crb). **77 Alamy Stock Photo:** Bob Daemmrich (crb). **NASA:** Johnson Space Center (cb, fcrb). **80–81 NASA:** Johnson Space Center. **81 NASA:** Johnson Space Center (bc). **82–83 ESA. 82 ESA:** (cb). **83 Getty Images:** Sebastien Salom-Gomis / AFP (tc, tr, c, cr). **NASA:** (bc). **84–85 NASA:** Johnson Space Center. **84 NASA. 85 Alamy Stock Photo:** Marc Fairhurst (cr). **Getty Images:** Yoshikazu Tsuno / AFP (br). **NASA:** Johnson Space Center (tc, bl); (crb). **86–87 ESA:** NASA. **86 NASA:** Johnson Space Center (clb). **88–89 NASA:** Johnson Space Center (c). **88 Japan Aerospace Exploration Agency (JAXA):** (cl, cr). **NASA:** (c); Johnson Space Center (clb, cb, crb). **89 Getty Images:** Red Huber / Orlando Sentinel / Tribune News Service (br). **NASA:** Johnson Space Center (tr). **90–91 NASA:** (t). **90 NASA:** (b). **91 Alamy Stock Photo:** NASA / UPI (bc). **NASA:** (cl, br); Johnson Space Center / Josh Valcarce (bl). **92–93 NASA:** Johnson Space Center. **93 NASA:** Johnson Space Center (ca, bc). **94–95 ESA:** NASA (b). **95 NASA:** Johnson Space Center (tr). **96–97 ESA:** NASA (t). **96 ESA:** NASA (br). **NASA:** Johnson Space Center (tl). **97 ESA:** NASA (bl). **NASA:** Johnson Space Center (br). **98–99 NASA:** Johnson Space Center. **98 ESA:** CNES / J-P. Haigner (bl). **100–101 Alamy Stock Photo:** NASA / UPI (c). **100 ESA:** NASA (clb). **NASA:** Johnson Space Center (tl). **101 NASA:** (br). **102–103 ESA:** NASA (b). **102 NASA:** Shane Kimbrough (bl). **103 NASA:** Johnson Space Center (tl); ESA (tr). **104–105 NASA:** (c). **105 Alamy Stock Photo:** NASA Photo (tr). **ESA:** NASA (br). **NASA:** (cr). **106 NASA:** Johnson Space Center. **107 ESA:** NASA (bc). **NASA:** Johnson Space Center (c). **108 NASA:** Johnson Space Center (tr, bl, br). **109 ESA:** NASA (tr). **NASA:** (cl); Johnson Space Center (c, bc). **112 NASA:** Johnson Space Center (tl, br). **113 Dreamstime.com:** Feathercollector (cr). **ESA:** NASA (cla). **NASA:** (tr); Johnson Space Center (bl); Johnson Space Center / SpaceX (br). **114 ESA:** (tl); NASA (cla). **NASA:** Johnson Space Center (cb); ESA (crb). **Science Photo Library:** NASA / Robert Markowitz (bl). **115 NASA:** Johnson Space Center. **116 NASA:** Johnson Space Center (tr). **116–117 NASA:** (b). **117 NASA:** Kennedy Space Center / Ben Smegelsk (tl); Johnson Space Center (tc, tr, ftr); Kennedy Space Center (cla); (cl). **118 NASA:** (tl); Johnson Space Center (bl). **118–119 NASA:** (c). **119 NASA:** Johnson Space Center (br, cr, cra); (bc). **120–121 Alamy Stock Photo:** NASA Photo (tc). **120 ESA:** David Gerhardt (bc). **NASA:** Johnson Space Center (br). **121 Alamy Stock Photo:** Vital Archive (br). **Dorling Kindersley:** Dreamstime.com (bc). **NASA:** Kennedy Space Center / Ben Smegelsky (tl). **122 Getty Images:** Ivan Couronne / AFP (tl). **Dr Suzie Imber:** (br). **122–123 NASA:** Kennedy Space Center (tc). **123 Getty Images:** Liz Hafalia / The San Francisco Chronicl (bl). **NASA:** Kennedy Space Center (tr). **124–125 NASA:** Johnson Space Center. **124 NASA:** Johnson Space Center (cl). **126 NASA:** (cr); Johnson Space Center (bl). **127 NASA:** (tr, tc, c, cl); Johnson Space Center (br). **Smithsonian National Air and Space Museum:** (bc). **128–129 NASA. 129 NASA:** Johnson Space Center (br). **130–131 NASA:** Johnson Space Center. **131 NASA:** Johnson Space Center (bc). **132–133 NASA:** Johnson Space Center. **132 NASA:** Johnson Space Center (ca); (bl). **Science Photo Library:** NASA (br). **134 Alamy Stock Photo:** (tr); Imaginechina Limited (bc); Newscom (br). **NASA:** Johnson Space Center (cra); (clb). **135 NASA:** (tr, cla); Johnson Space Center (cra, bl). **136 NASA:** Johnson Space Center (cl); (clb). **136–137 ESA:** NASA. **138 NASA:** Bill Ingalls (c); JSC (bc, br). **138–139 ESA:** NASA / B. Ingall (tr). **139 ESA:** Stephane Corvaja (bl); M. Pedoussaut (bc). **Getty Images:** Bill Ingalls / NASA (br). **NASA:** Bill Ingalls (clb). **142–143 NASA. 143 ESA:** DLR (bc). **NASA:** Bill Stafford and Robert Markowitz (cb, c). **144–145 ESA:** Karl Shreeve. **144 Alamy Stock Photo:** NASA Image Collection (clb). **NASA:** (bl). **146 Alamy Stock Photo:** Wirestock, Inc. (bl). **Blue Origin:** (cl). **Getty Images:** Mark Greenberg / Virgin Galactic (cla). **146–147 Getty Images:** Jean-Louis Atlan / Paris Match. **147 Axiom Space, Inc.:** (cb, br). **148–149 Inspiration4:** John Kraus (b). **149 Inspiration4:** (tl); Jared Isaacma (br). **Shutterstock.com:** SpaceX / UPI (tr). **SpaceX:** (tc). **150–151 NASA:** Johnson Space Center / Alberto Bertoli. **150 NASA:** (clb). **151 NASA:** Emmett Given (bc). **Sierra Space Corporation / Sierra Nevada Corporation:** (br, cb). **152–153 NASA. 152 Alamy Stock Photo:** Jon Arnold Images Ltd (bl). **154 Alamy Stock Photo:** eye35.pix (clb); Michael Ventura (tr); Nathan Willock-VIEW (bc); Xinhua (br). **155 Alamy Stock Photo:** EDU Vision (clb); ITAR-TASS News Agency (cla). **ESA:** (tr, cra).

Cover images: *Front:* **Alamy Stock Photo:** Andrey Armyagov; *Back:* **Dreamstime.com:** Ihor Svetiukha; **NASA:** (c, b), Robert Markowitz (t); *Spine:* Alamy Stock Photo: Andrey Armyagov.

Endpaper images: *Back:* **Dreamstime.com:** Ihor Svetiukha.

All other images © Dorling Kindersley.

For further information see: www.dkimages.com.

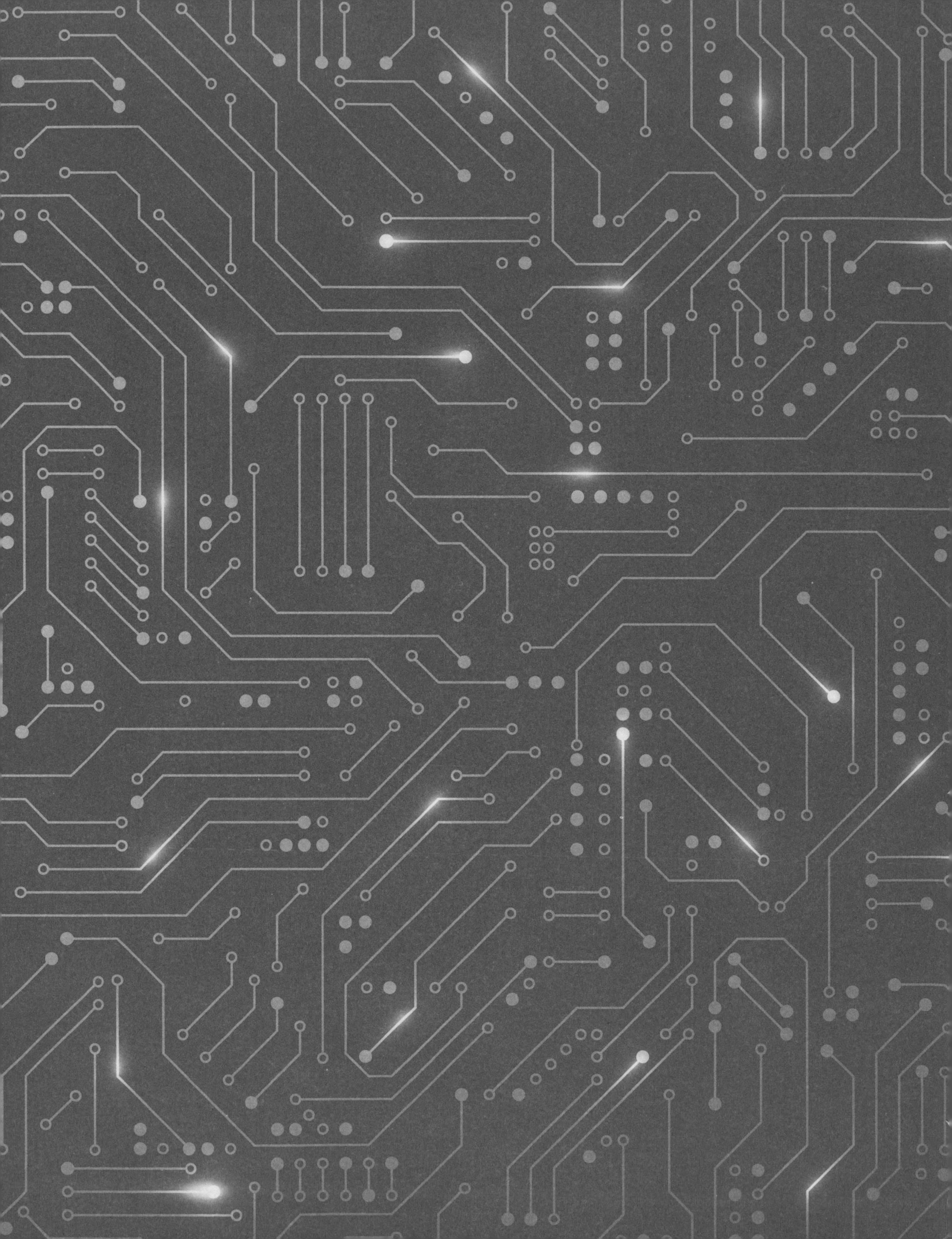